Envisioning India's Role in the Indo-Pacific

Centre for Security Studies

The field of Security Studies is vast and robust, situated within an ever-changing geopolitical and strategic landscape, where new dimensions are being added to the arena every day. At the Centre for Security Studies (CSS), we believe that the various factors and aspects influencing security must be better understood to fully and fairly gauge and examine their effect on contemporary international politics and security. CSS takes a unique, multidisciplinary approach to understanding and analysing security-related issues through in-depth analysis, reports, and policy briefs, which explore regional and thematic topics in the broader field of International Security Studies. Moreover, as the fields of International Relations and International Security have largely been western dominated disciplines, CSS aims to introduce newer perspectives from the Global South to the problems of security. Through this, we work towards aiding intellectuals and policymakers in their task of formulating more comprehensive security policies and strategies that are rooted in a deeper understanding of global dynamics.

The Centre for Security Studies is a student led research Centre, under the aegis of Jindal School of International Affairs, at O.P Jindal Global University.

CSS Security Series 1

Envisioning India's Role in the Indo-Pacific

Pankaj K Jha
Kritika S Karmakar
Joseph Punnen
Grace Cheema
Medha Nibhanupudi

SHIPRA

₹ 595; US$ 24.00
ISBN: 978-93-88691-74-1

First Published in India in 2021

Envisioning India's Role in the Indo-Pacific

Published by:
SHIPRA PUBLICATIONS
LG 18-19, Pankaj Central Market
I.P. Ext., Patparganj, Delhi 110092, India
Tel.: +91 11 2223 5152/6152, 9650028065
E-mail: info@shiprapublication.com
www.shiprapublication.com

Contents

Introduction

Ever since the launch of India's 'Look East policy' in 1992, India has come a long way in terms of the changes directed towards its extended neighbourhood and also subscribed to the new concept of the Indo-Pacific. In recent years, the Indo-Pacific region has gained a great deal of international attention and rightly so. The region is conceptualized as a hub of global trade and energy supply, and given the shifting geopolitical focus, it enticed major powers. Over the past decade, the increasing maritime activities carried out by neighbouring states, not to mention their subsequent geo-political implications on the international community, make this region an essential domain. Nevertheless, bearing in mind India's preeminent position in the Indo-Pacific, it becomes inevitable for the nation to safeguard its interests in the region. This research study will take a look at the recent changes and strategies initiated by the Indian government towards the Indo-Pacific region, along with the various economic, multilateral and bilateral relations that could impact India's policies in the future. The study will also look into the various regional forums India is associated with and how India shapes its policies according to their actions. Based on the evaluation of the official statements made by India on the matter, the policies, initiatives and the nature of relations with nation states and regional institutions, recommendations to improve India's current measures regarding the Indo-Pacific will be made.

Keywords: Indo-Pacific, Indo-Pacific Ocean's Initiative (IPOI), QUAD-Quadrilateral Security Dialogue, ASEAN, Indo-Pacific Division, Maritime domain, Blue economy, IORA

1 India's Indo-Pacific Approach

In the post-Cold War era, India's launch of the Look East Policy in 1992 under the Narasimha Rao government started off as a foreign policy initiative which primarily focused on forging political connections, increasing economic integration, and building security cooperation with Southeast Asian nations. To a certain extent the underlying objectives of India's current Indo-Pacific strategy remains more or less the same, with some revisions made over the years. As India's strategy towards the Indo-Pacific has been mostly centred around creating partnerships with other nations, considering China's assertive role in the region in the recent past, there has been a need for India to lay more importance on the Indo-Pacific than ever before. China's surging dominance and increased political and economic ventures with other nations of South Asia has altered the security environment of the region. Additionally, China's activities have not gone unnoticed by its rival, the US, and it too has found ways to make inroads in the region, to counter China. India's geographical location allows it to perceive the Indo-Pacific as a theatre of opportunities in order to pursue more partnerships but at the same time has placed it at a key position to play a better role in integrating the region whilst countering China and safeguarding its interests. The nation realizes this, and has started taking active steps in this direction.

The establishment of a new division, especially dedicated to the Indo-Pacific by the Ministry of External Affairs in April 2019, sheds light on the importance that India has started to place on the region. The document released by the Ministry states two reasons for the setting up of the division. Firstly, to integrate India's vision on the Indo-Pacific throughout the Government of India, "in line with the elements set out by the Prime Minister of India in June 2018". "Secondly, to provide substantive policy elements and programmes to that vision" (Ministry of External Affairs, 2020). Additionally, the division would handle matters related to the Indo-Pacific region and focus on integrating and partaking in the regional forums such as- IORA (Indian Ocean Rim Association), ASEAN (Association of Southeast Asian Nations), Mekong-Ganga Cooperation (MGC), East Asia Summit (EAS), Ayeyarwady-Chao Phraya-Mekong Economic Cooperation Strategy (ACMECS), and Asia-Europe Meeting (ASEM). "India calls for an open and inclusive order in the Indo-Pacific", and would adhere to the policy of 'ASEAN Centrality'. In addition to that, the document also highlights the need for collaboration with other states in the region and the need for peaceful resolution of conflicts through dialogues and negotiations, and respect for territorial sovereignty and integrity among nation-states.

The document also lists the various initiatives taken by India that have helped shape its current policy on the matter. One of these includes the Indo-Pacific Ocean's Initiative (IPOI) launched on November 4, 2019 by Prime Minister Narendra Modi, at the EAS in Bangkok, Thailand. The key focus of this initiative was "connectivity, maritime security, capacity building and resource sharing as well as the usage of the maritime domain more sustainably". It is based on shared values of cooperation, stability and promotion of peace and profitability in the region. A motivated partnership with 'like-minded' nations is at the core of the IPOI. In accordance with the proposition, such collaborations must have three common goals in the IOR (Indian Ocean Region) (where China is rapidly emerging as a dominant power), "namely wealth generation, welfare promotion and (cooperative) win-win strategies" (Panda, 2020). Apart from that during the launch India had also called for Vietnam for its participation in the initiative. During the India-Vietnam Business Forum, Secretary (East) of the MEA, Riva Ganguly Das, stated that Vietnam is a key pillar to India's 'Act East' policy, given their shared values and norms and their nature of relations with China ("Vietnam important for India's Indo-Pacific Ocean's Initiative: Senior diplomat", 2020).

From December 13–14, 2019, India hosted the Delhi Dialogue-XI, along with the ASEAN Member States on the theme "Advancing partnership in the Indo-Pacific". This was followed by the 6th Indian Ocean Dialogue with the Member States of IORA on the theme of- "Indo-Pacific: Re-imagining the Indian Ocean through an Expanded Geography". This was the first time "when two Track 1.5 dialogues—which are key elements of the Indian Ocean Rim Association (IORA), and the India-ASEAN calendars respectively—were held consecutively, and on similar, Indo-Pacific themes" (Ministry of External Affairs, 2019). The subject matter for both these events were centred around building the increasing recognition of the Indo-Pacific in academic and strategic circles. Lastly, from 6th to 7th February, 2020, India, in association with Australia and Indonesia, organised the 4th East Asia Summit (EAS) Conference on Maritime Security Cooperation in Chennai, India. The event saw the participation of over 100 participants from both academic and administrative positions and served as a platform for discussing several issues of maritime security cooperation and to devise useful suggestions on dealing with the challenges in the maritime domain, in a cooperative manner (Ministry of External Affairs, Media Centre, 2020). The document delved into five main regional forums that India intends to collaborate with more robustly. The following are the list of organizations-

- ***India and ASEAN***
  India's relations with ASEAN are primarily centred around connectivity, be it economic, socio-cultural, political or physical connectivity. The document by MEA, states that ASEAN is an important pillar of its foreign policy and the foundation of its Act East Policy (Ministry of External Affairs, 2020). Currently India and ASEAN have over 30 dialogue mechanisms concerning into various sectors. In an effort to increase connectivity via land, air and the sea among the ASEAN nations and India, India has launched the India-Myanmar-Thailand Trilateral Highway (IMT) project which intends to boost trade among the "ASEAN and India Free Trade Area, as well as the rest of Southeast Asia". The IMT trilateral highway project will be 1,360 km long, and will pass through the North-Eastern states of India. The project also aids to strengthen the Indian position as a counterbalance to the tactical influence of China in the region ("India-Myanmar-Thailand Trilateral Highway- Maritime Gateway", 2019). India has accelerated work on the bridges that are in Myanmar and also provided financial assistance for the same. Even Kaladan multi modal transport project is more than 90 per cent complete. Nevertheless, India is also interested in boosting its maritime connectivity with other ASEAN nations, for both economic and strategic purposes. Launching of more direct flights between Tier I and II cities of India and ASEAN countries is a proposal and

the ASEAN-India Maritime Transport Cooperation Agreement is being negotiated and finalized (Ministry of External Affairs, 2020).

Apart from that, India has a Free Trade Agreement (FTA) with ASEAN, and this sector has witnessed a steady growth, as ASEAN is the fourth largest trading partner of India at USD 96.79 billion. Both parties "have set the target of USD 200 billion by 2022" (Ministry of External Affairs, 2020). However, even though the document states that the investment has been substantial from both ends, the reality seems to be slightly different. From 1995 to 2016 Indian imports from ASEAN witnessed a robust growth of 12.3 percent while, on the other hand Indian exports to ASEAN recorded a CAGR (Compound Average Growth Rate) of 11.4 percent. "The total bilateral trade between India and ASEAN was to the tune of USD 86,862.32 million during 2019–20 compared to 96795.04 million during 2018–19 and India's total exports to the trade block was USD 31,492.51 million during 2019–20 among which India's engineering exports to the region amounted to US$ 10589.8 million" (https://farmmech.eepc.expoplatform.com/). This demonstrates that the balance of trade has been on the side of the ASEAN member countries throughout the reference period (Bhogal, 2020). Furthermore, India's decision to not join the Regional Comprehensive Economic Partnership (RCEP), might also affect India's trade relations with ASEAN. In light of this, India is seen reviewing the FTAs signed with ASEAN.

On August 29, 2020, the India- ASEAN Economic Ministers Consultations were held. During which Commerce and Industry Minister Piyush Goyal stated that India would engage in a review of the Free Trade Agreements, mainly the ASEAN- India Trade in Goods Agreement (AITGA), with 10 member states of ASEAN (Mitra & Srinivas, 2020). The Prime Minister too has called for an 'early review' of the (AITGA), expressing the "importance of diversification and resilience of supply chains for post-COVID economic recovery" (Haidar, 2020). As an alternative to RCEP, India will attempt to better its bilateral ties with its Southeast Asian counterparts. It will be done by shoring up existing minilateral organisations where India can take up a leadership role, similar to the the Bay of Bengal Initiative for Multi-Sectoral Technical and Economic Cooperation (BIMSTEC), where "Thailand and Myanmar are members, and Mekong-Ganga Cooperation, with a view towards actively engaging Vietnam" (Izzuddin, 2020).

In addition to that, India also aims to improve its "people-to-people connectivity" with the member states of ASEAN. This includes targeting the tourism sector as well as initiating programmes and projects for capacity building among states. "Regular exchanges take place between the ASEAN Connectivity Coordinating Committee (ACCC) and India on Connectivity. Prime Minister Narendra Modi announced a line of credit of $1 billion for facilitating projects in connectivity at the 13th ASEAN-India Summit in 2015" (Ministry of External Affairs, n.d.).

In terms of tourism, the year 2019 was lauded as the "ASEAN-India Year of tourism", in order to reinforce the two-way flow of tourists. With regards to the space sector, "ISRO is implementing a project proposal for (i) establishment of Tracking and Data Reception Station and Data Processing Facility at Ho Chi Minh City; (ii) up-gradation of Tracking Telemetry and Command (TTC) Centre at Biak, Indonesia; and (iii) Training of ASEAN Personnel in Space Science and Technology at the Centre for Space Science and Technology Education in Asia and the Pacific (CSSTEAP)" (Ministry of External Affairs, n.d.).

In accordance with the concept of ASEAN centrality, the East Asia Summit (EAS)d was established in 2005. The forum allows primary players of the Asia-Pacific to deliberate over issues of common concerns in a peaceful and transparent manner. As one of the founding members of the initiative, India has engaged and utilised the forum to actualise its Indo-Pacific Strategy and form strategic partnerships on various fronts with its fellow members.

- ***EAS (East Asia Summit)***

  At the 14th East Asia Summit in Bangkok, held on 4th November, 2019, Prime Minister Narendra Modi announced India's Indo-Pacific Oceans Initiative (IPOI). In his address, Prime Minister Modi, mentioned that the IPOI will be in line with the "Sustainable Development Goal 14" which stresses on the need to "conserve and sustainably use the maritime domain" (Ministry of External Affairs Media Centre, 2019). This includes maintaining the ecological balance of the waters by reducing pollution and making a conscious effort to maintain resources. The importance of the ASEAN-Outlook was also highlighted during the summit. The 4th EAS conference on Maritime Security Cooperation was jointly hosted by India, Australia and Indonesia on the 6–7th of February, 2020. The goal of the EAS Conference was to share India's concept with its fellow member countries and to understand the various perspectives of the other nations on multiple issues of maritime security cooperation and to come up with suggestions on tackling challenges in the maritime domain in a cooperative manner (Prasad, 2020).

Moreover, India has been attempting to strengthen its economic integration with its Southeast and East Asian counterparts. Apart from using the ASEAN platform, India has also been able to better its relations with the nations of the Mekong region, primarily due to its association with the Mekong-Ganga Cooperation (MGC). Based on political and cultural lines, MGC enables India to form closer ties with states "on the basis of socio-cultural alliances", thereby opening up opportunities for both India and the Mekong nations.

- ***Mekong-Ganga Cooperation (MGC)***

An initiative by the six countries, which comprises India and the five ASEAN nations, the Mekong-Ganga Cooperation (MGC) facilitates the collaboration on sectors of tourism, culture, education, as well as transport and communications, among all the six of its member states (Ministry of External Affairs, 2017). This cooperation also reinforces the idea of physical and cultural connectivity. India hosted the 6th MGC Ministerial Meeting on 4th September, 2012, during which the "India-CLMV Quick Impact Projects (QIP) Fund was established, along with the announcement of setting up a Working Group on Health for sharing information and cooperation for pandemics management and a Common Archival Resource Centre (CARC) at the Nalanda University" (Ministry of External Affairs, 2016).

The India-MGC quick impact scheme "focuses on projects of a short gestation period that could directly benefit the local communities, with results that are immediate and visible". Moreover, an annual contribution of USD 1 million is made by the "India-CLMV Quick Impact Projects (QIP) Revolving Fund" (Ministry of External Affairs Media Centre, 2012). 24 projects have been completed so far, which include – "15 in Cambodia and 9 in Viet Nam and 11 projects in Cambodia; 4 in Vietnam and 3 in Lao PDR are currently under implementation" (Ministry of External Affairs, 2020). It is speculated that India will launch more QIPs in Southeast Asia in the future.

As part of the cultural initiative undertaken by India, in 2014, India established the "MGC Asian Traditional Textile Museum in Siem Reap, Cambodia". The museum showcases the range of textile traditions from India and the Mekong delta, thereby making use of soft power to strengthen relations between India and the ASEAN nations. Furthermore, on August 1, 2019, the 10th MGC Foreign Ministers' Meeting was organized in Bangkok, Thailand, which saw the adoption of a new MGC Plan of Action (POA) (2019–2022). As per this POA, the project foresees cooperation in mainly seven sectors of – "tourism and culture, education, public health and traditional medicine, agriculture and allied sectors, transport and communication, MSMEs as well as three new areas of cooperation, i.e. water resources management, science and technology, skill development and capacity building" (Ministry of External Affairs Media Center, 2019). India also proposed to develop a website of MGC that would contain information on the various joining programmes and activities. Apart from that, India has also made significant contributions in terms of capacity building and human resource development by cooperating in the educational sector and offering various scholarship schemes. At the MGC, India seems to be taking active steps to expand its sphere of influence over its East Asian neighbours.

Another platform that allows India to better engage with its East Asian counterparts is that of Ayeyawady-Chao Phraya-Mekong Economic Cooperation Strategy (ACMECS). India became a part of ACMECS in 2019, as a "development partner" along with Australia, Japan, South Korea, China and the US. India's ability to garner more allies for its Indo-Pacific vision is not simply limited to its bilateral relations but also extends to the sub regional and multiregional forums. ACMECS provides India with an opportunity to facilitate better trade and investment relations with other regional actors.

- ***Ayeyawady-Chao Phraya-Mekong Economic Cooperation Strategy (ACMECS)***

  "Established in 2003, the ACMECS is a cooperation framework among Cambodia, Lao People's Democratic Republic, Myanmar, Thailand, and Viet Nam, which is aimed at increasing cooperation at three fronts- connectivity, trade and investment and environment and human resource cooperation". In July 2019, Thailand invited India to join the ACMECS as a "Development Partner" alongside China, Australia, Republic of Korea, Japan and USA. At the 10th Mekong Ganga Cooperation Ministerial Meeting, India stressed on the importance of connectivity among these nation states and on the need for an early completion of the "India-Myanmar-Thailand Trilateral Highway" along with its extension to

Cambodia, Laos and Vietnam ("Fillip to "Act East" as India joins key sub-regional group", 2019). Also, India mentioned the need to finalize the India-Myanmar-Thailand Motor Vehicle Agreement, which would provide a faster route for movement of goods and aid in both trade and tourism. Bearing in mind the emphasis laid on connectivity, a Line of Credit of USD 1 billion, that would aid in the connectivity projects that India embarked on with the ASEAN nations, was proposed by India.

In addition to being a part of ACMECS, India is also a member of the IORA (Indian Ocean Rim Association). This forum was set up on the "lines of shared democratic values among the Asian nations" and aimed to expand cooperation on issues such as trade, investment, fisheries and cultural cooperation. The organisation mainly consists of nations that share boundaries with the Indian Ocean. Given India's commanding presence in the region, India's association with the organization is essential as it extends to nations beyond Southeast Asia. An active role played in the forum will enable India to expand on its vision on the Indo-Pacific.

- ***Indian Ocean Rim Association (IORA)***

  "The Indian Ocean Rim Association (IORA) has identified six Priority Areas (Academic, Science and Technology, Fisheries Management, Tourism and Cultural Exchanges, Disaster Risk Management, Maritime Safety and Security, Trade and Investment Facilitation) and 2 Cross-cutting Issues (Blue Economy and Women's Economic Empowerment) for regional cooperation" (Ministry of External Affairs, 2020). As of now, India is one of the leading nations in the sectors of Science and Technology Cooperation and Disaster Risk Management and Academic. Additionally, it is also a part of the cluster group for Blue Economy and Women's Economic Empowerment as well as Tourism, Maritime Safety and Security. Apart from that, India also actively participates and hosts events based on capacity building. From 28–29 November, 2019, the Ministry of External Affairs and the Federation of Indian Commerce and Industries (FICCI), in collaboration with the Indian Ocean Rim Association (IORA) hosted the second Somalia-Yemen-Development-program (SYDP-II). The aim of the workshop was to enhance knowledge and capacities of participants to improve the values and quality of fish products by implementing simple technologies and method, for developing small-scale fisheries activities and business ("Second SYDP

(SYDP-II) Workshop on Improving the Quality and Value of Fisheries Products for Food Security, Coastal Livelihoods – Indian Ocean Rim Association – IORA", n.d.). In 2019, the 19th IORA Council of Ministers Meeting was held at Abu Dhabi, where V. Muraleedharan, Minister of State for External Affairs, mentioned that "India plans to host a workshop on beach and cruise tourism in the spring of 2020 in partnership with its business chambers" ("Indian Ocean Rim Association discusses ways to achieve larger cooperation", 2019). Additionally, India is one of the biggest contributors to the IORA special fund, and "as of 2019 has made a contribution of USD 1 million to the fund" ("Indian Ocean Rim Association discusses ways to achieve larger cooperation | | Factly", 2019).

In recent years, there has been an escalating interest in the Indian Ocean Region as well as in the Indo-Pacific, by European nations. As per the policy guidelines released by Germany, it mentions that Germany wants to "promote a European Indo-Pacific strategy". (Aneja, 2020) Nations like France and Australia too have expressed similar interests. All these countries are a part of the Asia-Europe Meeting which provides a platform for both the Asian and European powers to collaborate on various issues. India can use this forum to better engage with its European counterparts and expand on its vision of the Indo-Pacific whilst reducing the economic dependency on China, which has been a cause of concern for many European nations.

- ***Asia Europe Meeting***

"The Asia-Europe Meeting (ASEM) is an intergovernmental process that fosters dialogue and cooperation between Asia and Europe. ASEM addresses political, economic, social, cultural, and educational issues of common interest, in a spirit of mutual respect and equal partnership" ("About ASEM and ASEM Education", n.d.). Currently it "consists of 53 partners - 30 European and 21 Asian countries", including the ASEAN and the European Union (EU). India joined ASEM in 2008. "India's first Summit level participation was at the 7th Summit held in Beijing from 24–25 October 2008, where former Prime Minister, Shri Manmohan Singh led the Indian delegation" (Ministry of External Affairs, 2017).

Moreover, India organized the 11th ASEM Foreign Ministers Meeting from 11-12 November, 2013 in Delhi. The theme for this meeting was "ASEM: Bridge to partnership for growth and development" ("11th ASEM Foreign Ministers' Meeting (FMM11) • ASEM InfoBoard", 2013). The Foreign Ministers' Meeting is essential for the overall cooperation of the ASEM process. India has been an active participant of the forum since its admission. For the past five years, it has been conducting special courses for the ASEM diplomats at the Foreign Service Institute. An another area where India works closely with ASEM is in the sector of Customs cooperation.

Apart from these economic and political initiatives, India has also joined a quasi-defence partnership which is known as Quad. Even though it is a loose collaboration, it is viewed as a critical counter to the Chinese strategy and its aggressively expansionist policies. India's association with the Quad enables it to engage with other actors beyond its immediate ASEAN counterparts. For India, Ind0-Pacific and Quad are two parallel concepts which need not be synchronised to gain maximum advantage.

2 Quad-Quadrilateral Security Dialogue

After the initial failure of the Quadrilateral Security Dialogue also known as the Quad in 2008, the concept made a brief appearance in the form of "Democratic Security Dialogue" during the Japanese Prime Minister Shinzo Abe's speech in 2012. Even though not much came to be of it at the time, this set the foundation for Quad 2.0. The Quadrilateral Security Dialogue is an informal strategic forum between India, US, Japan and Australia. The main aim of the Quad has been to secure the Indo-Pacific, ideally to curb the surging influence of China in the region. India's involvement in the league of such major democratic nations, provides India with an opportunity to not only actualize its intentions in the region but also strategically parry China's advances. Prime Minister Narendra Modi's 2018 address at the Shangri la dialogue, outlined India's policy towards the Indo-Pacific and laying a special emphasis on the fact that India does not aim to counter China and maintains a position of ASEAN centrality. However, the Quad sees the assembly of major powers and could be a significant forum for India to develop multilateral and bilateral relations with other stakeholders in the region.

On 12th November, 2017, the four nations took part in formal official level discussions at Manila, Philippines, at the margins of the 31st ASEAN and the 12th East Asian Summit. This was considered to be the first meeting after over a decade that revived the functioning of the Quad. As per the press release made by the Indian Ministry of External Affairs following the meeting, the "discussions were focused on cooperation, promotion of peace, stability and prosperity in the region and agreed upon the need for a 'free, open, prosperous and inclusive' Indo-Pacific" (Ministry of External Affairs Media Centre,

2017). Furthermore, they addressed common concerns on terrorism and proliferation linkages that affect the region and ways to enhance connectivity. From 2017 to 2019, the four nations met over five times. The 2017 meeting was followed by two meetings in 2018, the first one being held in June at Singapore. The second meeting saw an emphasis on "rule-based order" and ASEAN centrality. The inclusion of "rule-based order" was primarily done to combat China's aggressive stance in the South China Sea. However, India is the only country within the Quad that merely mentioned that it would promote rule-based order, unlike its other counterparts who stated that they would 'uphold and strengthen the rules-based order ("Quad Meets Again, Discusses Rules-Based Order in 'Inclusive' Indo-Pacific", 2018)'.

Given India's close proximity to China and the constant border tensions between the two, India's exclusion of the concept seems justified. As per the statement made by the Ministry of External Affairs after the meeting, "the four nations reaffirmed their strong support for ASEAN centrality and ASEAN-led mechanisms in the regional architecture for the Indo-Pacific" (Ministry of External Affairs, 2018). In addition to that, agreements to partner with other nations and institutions through plurilateral formats were also made. The third round of meeting held in November of 2018 also witnessed the similar stress on objectives of regional security, counter-terrorism, non-proliferation, maritime cooperation, connectivity and development as inclusivity and engagement of ASEAN and other regional forums (Ministry of External Affairs, 2018). In 2019, the Quad saw its first Ministerial Meeting in May of that year in Bangkok. Apart from touching upon common objectives of "ASEAN centrality, regional security, maritime cooperation and humanitarian assistance and disaster relief" (Ministry of External Affairs, 2019), it is also believed that the four democracies explored alternatives to China's Belt and Road Initiative (BRI) (Chaudhury, 2019).

- ***Quad Plus***

  Considering the pandemic of 2020, the interactions carried out among the members of Quad have mainly occurred virtually. However, this new modem also witnessed the presence of three new nations in the discussions. On 20th March, 2020, the first Quad-plus video conference was initiated by the US. This meeting included the participation of New Zealand, Vietnam and South Korea (Bagchi, 2020). As per the statement issued by the Ministry of External Affairs, "the participants shared their assessments of the current situation with respect to COVID-19, and discussed ways to synergize their efforts to counter its spread." (Ministry of External Affairs, 2020). During the second Vice- Ministerial Virtual meeting in the same month, the nations also discussed ways to manage the economic repercussions of the pandemic, collectively. But, given the nature of discussions of the Quad Plus dialogues, it is anticipated that the nations would solely focus on the pandemic and might shift from their original objective of increasing inclusivity in the Indo-Pacific and countering China. Furthermore, in October 2020, the four democracies met in Tokyo for the second Quadrilateral Ministerial Meeting where India met with each of its counterparts bilaterally.

With respect to military exercises carried out in the region, India has been engaging in the MALABAR exercises with the US and Japan since the 1990's. However, it was only in 2020, when Australia was also invited to join the same. Nevertheless, previously India had been reluctant to expand the format of maritime exercises to Australia, given China's constant interruptions and bilateral relations with Australia. Bearing in mind that these exercises will be taking place off the coast of the Visakhapatnam in the Bay of Bengal, in the Indian Ocean, it will send out a strong statement to China. In 2007 Singapore took part in the MALABAR naval exercises. However, involvement of other regional nations in the same have not been seen yet. Considering the fact that China has been attempting to cultivate better relations with Myanmar and Bangladesh, as well as strengthened its military cooperation with Sri Lanka over the past decade, in order to gain access to the Bay of Bengal and Indian Ocean. Thus, it becomes imperative for India to engage such regional powers to safeguard its interests in the Indo Pacific.

The Quad plus requires to include Indonesia, Singapore and Philippines also into the structure as it is critical because of their geographic vantage locations.

3 Outlining India's Role in the Indo-Pacific

The US's proposal to India to become a part of the Quad, is a clear sign that the US views India as an important stakeholder in the region. Apart from that, India's geographical location allows the US to gain better access to the region. The US has also recognized India as a major defence partner. India too has made use of this acknowledgement and signed multiple defence agreements with the US including "LEMOA (Logistics Exchange Memorandum of Agreement), COMCASA (Communications Compatibility and Security Agreement), STA1 (Strategic Trade Authorization) and the Industrial Security Annex, as well as conducting the Tiger Triumph exercises and 2+2 dialogue" (Panda, 2020). Being associated with the US at so many forums give India a chance to engage with the nation better at multiple levels. However, India needs to be mindful of the alliance and how it will be perceived at the international front, especially with respect to China. Over the past decade, China's advances have not only been limited to the maritime domain but have also been seen on the Sino-Indian border. In addition to that, China has also made attempts to influence India's smaller neighbours like Myanmar and Nepal against India. India also faces a significant security threat from the CPEC (China- Pakistan Economic Corridor) initiative by China, as it passes through some sensitive regions of Jammu and Kashmir. Bearing these in mind, India needs to carefully weigh its alliances, so as to not aggravate China and also maintain its position on ASEAN centrality and inclusivity and should refrain from becoming a part of any power bloc.

Having initiated the concept of the Quadrilateral Security Dialogue on the lines of shared democratic values, Japan becomes an important stakeholder in the region. Japan's technological advancements can be an aid to India in terms of cybersecurity and development of artificial intelligence. Apart from being associated with the Quad, together India and Japan's relations were initially built on the common ground of strategic and global partnership. However, this alliance has come a long way from that since then. During the G-20 summit in 2019, Prime Minister Narendra Modi, organized a bilateral meeting with Japanese Prime Minister Shinzo Abe, where issues of mutual interest were discussed including "Japan's assistance to India for the coalition on disaster resilience infrastructure, fugitive economic offenders and anti-corruption measures, and infrastructure works of Japanese companies in the North East" (Ministry of External Affairs, n.d.). Apart from that India is also a part of the Defence Ministers Meeting, NSA-level Dialogue, 2+2 dialogues and FOC Consultations. Nevertheless, India's vision of the Indo Pacific also includes Africa and considering that both the nations have envisioned the "Platform for Japan-India Business cooperation in Asia-Africa Region" (Panda, 2020) provides India with an opportunity to better expand its relations with the African nations with the help of Japan.

With regards to the Quad, even though India enjoys good relations with both the US and Japan, its relations with Australia have been slightly strained. Australia itself has been cautious with its moves and given its relations with China, and the level of influence China exerts on Australia, the island nation was forced to back out of Quad 1.0. Even with regards to the Malabar naval exercises, initially India exhibited slight inhibitions when asked to invite Australia. However, the fact that India did take a step forward implies that there is a possibility of strengthening the India-Australia relationship. Apart from signing a framework on or security cooperation in 2014, India and Australia have also been expanding their relations on multilateral forums. This could be seen from 2015-2016, where India and Australia worked closely on establishing the Secretariat in Mauritius, and with Indonesia in the IORA (Indian Ocean Regional Association) (Jaishankar, 2020).

Apart from the US, Japan and Australia, India also needs to focus on Quad Plus, as it is a great way to engage regional actors and is in line with India's objective of inclusivity. However, this would imply that India should develop better bilateral relations with each of the ASEAN member states. In recent years, India has built stronger relations with Indonesia, which seems to be taking up the role of an unofficial leader at ASEAN. In 2014, India and Indonesia organized naval exercises and have also adopted the "Shared Vision in Maritime Cooperation on the Indo-Pacific" (Nagda, 2019). Considering that both the nations have been victims of China's armed forces, India at its borders and Indonesia with its conflicts near the Natuna islands; India could utilize this common problem in its favour and work towards developing a stronger defence cooperation with the nation.

However, it is essential to not forget the India's other neighbours, such as Myanmar, Nepal and Sri Lanka. Even though relatively weaker states, they are the most susceptible to China's debt trap diplomacy. In order to counter China's economic advances and considering its role as a security provider, India with the help of its fellow Quad members could provide an alternative to these states. This would aid to keep in check the rising influence of China in the region. However, bearing in mind that India's association with the Quad is based on the shared foundation of democratic principles, India should also employ this concept to garner the support of other democracies as well. Britain's proposal of a 5G club of 10 democratic nations, including India is a good way to build better connectivity and bilateral relations with other Western nations. "As per the D-10 proposal put forward by the UK, it would include the US, Italy, Germany, France, Japan and Canada – plus Australia, South Korea and India. This was primarily set up to provide alternatives to suppliers of 5G equipment and other technologies without relying on China" (Khanna, 2020). This step was largely motivated by the ban on Huawei and suspicions surrounding Chinese espionage and surveillance activities. India's involvement at such platforms would not only provide an opportunity for better technological collaborations and exchange among states but will also aid in utilizing similar technologies in its maritime defence equipment to better secure its naval borders.

India would also have to look into the Blue Dot network to look for synergising its efforts with the other three Quad partners. While Blue Dot network is still in preliminary stages but the possibility of convergence between Indo-Pacific Economic Corridor and Blue Dot network would offer many possibilities in integrating the two regions of South and Southeast Asia together. India's IPOI proposal is one such converging point.

4 India and the Indo-Pacific Oceans Initiative (IPOI)

The concept of the Indo- Pacific Oceans Initiative (IPOI) was first introduced by Prime Minister, Narendra Modi in 2019 at the 14th East Asia Summit. In light of the ASEAN's Outlook and the EAS statement for Partnership on Sustainability, the initiative was proposed as a cooperative effort to secure the region (Ministry of External Affairs, 2019). The Prime Minister stated that the "IPOI is in line with Sustainable Development Goal- 14, which aims to conserve and sustainably use the maritime domain". He highlighted the need to develop better institutional roots so as to overcome global challenges. On the side-line of the EAS, the Prime Minister also held discussions with the Prime Minister of Vietnam and Japan. In his conversation with Japanese Prime Minister, Shinzo Abe, both the leaders evaluated the evolving security environment of the Indo-Pacific and agreed to strengthen bilateral cooperation for "peace, prosperity and development in the region" (Chaudhury, 2019).

Moreover, on 12th November, 2020, the Ministry of External Affairs of India made a press release on the 17th India-ASEAN summit. This was one more event where the Prime Minister shed light on the IPOI and expressed the importance of ASEAN and other ASEAN led forums for India's vision for the Indo-Pacific. Furthermore, the Prime Minister also drew many similarities between the ASEAN Outlook and IPOI, and stressed upon India's position of ASEAN centrality and the role played by the Security and Growth of All in the region (SAGAR). In light of the COVID-19 pandemic, an announcement of the contribution of USD 1 million to the COVID-19 ASEAN Response Fund was also made (Ministry of External Affairs; Media Centre, 2020).

The notion of the IPOI has also been extended to other nations in the region, and this has led to many bilateral negotiations with these states. At the 17th India-Vietnam Joint commission meeting India invited Vietnam to collaborate on one of the seven pillars of IPOI, in addition to enhancing bilateral relations in line with IPOI by India and ASEAN's Outlook on the Indo Pacific (Ministry of External Affairs; Media Centre, 2020). "At the Joint Declaration on a Shared Vision for Maritime Cooperation in the Indo- Pacific between India and Australia in June, 2020, it was discussed that in light of the IPOI, both the nations will work together bilaterally, regionally and multilaterally to work towards common goals of preserving maritime ecology, reducing the impact of maritime pollution (especially plastics), maritime security, sustainable use of marine resources; capacity building and resource sharing; disaster risk reduction and management; science, technology and academic cooperation; and trade, connectivity and maritime transport" (Ministry of External Affairs, 2020). Other domains of the issue such as sharing of information bilaterally, strengthening navy to navy cooperation was also touched upon.

Apart from the statements and bilateral arrangements made by the Prime Minister and the Minister of External Affairs, Subramanian Jaishankar, the IPOI and India's vision on the Indo-Pacific has been emphasized at many other forums. At the Foreign Secretary's Speech at Policy Exchange in UK held on 3rd of November, 2020, Foreign Secretary of India, H.E Harsh Vardhan Shringla (Ministry of External Affairs, India, 2020), mentioned that the "Indian Ministry has set up the Indo-Pacific division as well as an Oceania division". Furthermore, he stated the seven pillars of the IPOI and shed light on "India's aspirations on securing end-to-end supply chains in the region through SAGAR, so as to minimize disproportionate dependence on a single country and ensure prosperity for all stakeholder nations" (Ministry of External Affairs, Media Centre, 2020). India's foreign policy perspective, even though focused on the Indo-Pacific, is not simply limited to it. It also intends to assimilate its policy and actions so as to synchronize with its larger interest in Southeast Asia and Oceania as well as to build better engagements in East Asia.

5 India's Foreign Policy Perspective

India- ASEAN Relations

The relationship between India and the members of ASEAN are implemented through the Plan of Action (POA) which forms the basis for the execution of the ASEAN-India Partnership that is aimed at establishing peace, progress and shared prosperity. Such precedents were established in the last decades beginning with the 2004 talks in Laos, followed by the "Vision Statement of the ASEAN-India Commemorative Summit on 20 December, 2012 in New Delhi, India; and the Delhi Declaration of the ASEAN-India Commemorative Summit to Mark the 25th Anniversary of ASEAN-India Dialogue Relations on 25 January, 2018 in New Delhi, India and the recently concluded Plan of Action (POA) of 2021-25."

Through the application of POA, India and ASEAN will also work towards supporting the ASEAN Community building and integration process, this includes the ASEAN 2025: "Forging Ahead Together", "aimed at a politically cohesive, economically integrated, socially responsible and a truly people-oriented, people-centred and rules-based ASEAN, narrowing the development gap and enhancing ASEAN Connectivity". Both India and ASEAN will also further promote collaboration in addressing common and emerging challenges as well as promote coordination in other international fora on issues of collective concern to contribute to overall peace, prosperity and stability. After the 34th ASEAN Summit in Bangkok, it has established the precedents for cooperation between India and ASEAN through the existing ASEAN-led mechanisms in the four key areas outlined in the Outlook, "namely (i) maritime cooperation, (ii) connectivity, (iii) UN

Sustainable Development Goals (SDGs) 2030, and (iv) economic and other possible areas of cooperation to contribute to peace, prosperity and development in the region."

The 20th ASEAN-India Joint Cooperation Committee Meeting came at a time marked by the COVID-19 pandemic, leading to a disruption in the global supply chains resulting in the decline of economies around the world and the relations between the United States and China coming to an all-time low resulting in the tensions in South China Sea. During the meeting which was held via a video conference, both India and ASEAN "reaffirmed their commitment to further strengthen and deepen their cooperation." Both sides noted the progress made for the implementation of the ASEAN-India Plan of Action (2016-2020), and "shared their commitment to complete the development of the new Plan of Action for 2021-2025 to further strengthen their strategic partnership over the next five years." ("ASEAN, India strengthen cooperation - ASEAN | One Vision One Identity One Community", 2020)

The COVID-19 pandemic, was something that both India and the ASEAN member states had to keep in mind while framing the Plan of Action for the next five years and both sides have conveyed their intentions to fight the pandemic together. India's Prime Minister Narendra Modi has engaged in telephonic conversations with the leaders of Indonesia, Myanmar, Thailand, Singapore, and Vietnam on ways to tackle the pandemic together. The The ASEAN-India Ministerial Meet was co-chaired by India's External Affairs Minister Dr. S. Jaishankar and Thailand's Foreign Affairs Minister Don Pramudwinai with the aim to review the status of ASEAN-India Strategic Partnership concerning several areas, "including maritime cooperation, connectivity, education & capacity building and people-to-people contacts". The implementation of the ASEAN-India Plan of Action (2016-2020), was also reviewed in the meet. "The meeting also assessed the preparations for the upcoming 17th ASEAN-India Summit and the progress in the implementation of key decisions of the Leaders of ASEAN Member States (AMS) and India arrived at the 16th ASEAN-India Summit held in Bangkok in November 2019 and the previous Summits." (Ministry of External Affairs, Media Centre, 2020). As a result, in the new ASEAN-India Plan of Action (2021-2025) being adopted "envisages greater cooperation in areas ranging from trade to maritime security and counter-terrorism".

"The Plan of Action will help both the sides to work towards the ASEAN 2025 vision for an economically integrated and rules-based grouping that narrows the development gap and enhances connectivity".

Both sides are expected to collaborate to combat common challenges and to improve coordination at international organisations and platforms. The meeting also "reviewed the strategic partnership in several key areas such as the maritime cooperation, connectivity, and people-to-people contacts". Both the sides agreed that "as a premier leaders-led forum for dialogue and cooperation on broad strategic, political, and economic issues…. with the aim of promoting peace, stability and economic prosperity in the region" (ASEAN-India Plan of Action 2021-2025). It also led to an agreement on joint exercises and activities, and to improve the defence capabilities to counter the challenges arising from the "maritime domain, counter-terrorism, humanitarian assistance, disaster relief, peacekeeping operations, and cyber-security". Under the maritime security clause, both are committed to provide "freedom of navigation and overflight, unimpeded commerce, the non-use of force, and the resolution of disputes by peaceful means, in accordance with international law, including the 1982 UN Convention on the Law of the Sea (UNCLOS)". Regarding the economic aspects, both the sides are continuing to make ASEAN-India Free Trade Area (AIFTA) even more accessible and more trade-friendly by initiating a review of the ASEAN-India Trade in Goods Agreement and are focused on the ratification of the ASEAN-India Investment Agreement to facilitate further economic integration. Whereas, in the case of connectivity, both want to bring each other closer and promote physical connectivity by "completing the missing links between South and Southeast Asia, including, but not limited to, expediting the completion of relevant sections of the India-Myanmar-Thailand trilateral highway and supporting steps to build an economic corridor along it and its extension to Cambodia, Lao PDR, and Vietnam." (*Plan of Action of to Implement the ASEAN-India Partnership for Peace, Progress and Shared Prosperity (2016-2020), 2020) [Plan of Action to Implement the ASEAN-India Partnership for Peace, Progress and Shared Prosperity (2021-2025), 2020].*

Glimpses of India's Indo-Pacific Strategy at the Shangri-La Dialogue

The term Indo-Pacific was propounded by the likes of Japan, Australia and the United States, and many other Western nations much later, when New Delhi assumed to have a central role. It can also be argued that such a term came into existence due to the rise of China and its ever increasing economic, political, and military engagements all over the world, especially in Asia. This has forced the nations like Australia, Japan and the U.S. to completely revamp their strategic policies. Whereas, in the case of India it's engagement in the Indo-Pacific corresponds with the rise of China, especially in the Indian Ocean Region (IOR) and in South Asia. In spite of their differences in priorities, the rise of Beijing's presence across their backyard is a cause of concern for New Delhi, Washington, Tokyo and Canberra.

India has been moving ahead in the Indo-Pacific and does not wish to jeopardize the security of India, thereby India has to strike a balance between its developing geopolitical competition with China as well as its partnership with other nations of the West. Thus, India's strategy in the Indo-Pacific is seen as an opportunity to build up its presence while maintaining a strategic advantage to address its constraints in securing its interests. Following the end of the Cold War, there was no such strategic rivalry in the Indian Ocean and naturally India was able to play a dominant role and also ensure a favourable outcome for its tactical interests. However, the recent growth of China in the last decade and its encroachment into India's backyard has made the nation think twice before making another move. Such a notion made governments of both Dr. Manmohan Singh and Prime Minister Narendra Modi to review their foreign policy.

Due to the rising economic power of China, the country can offer better economic projects and assistance both financially and militarily to countries in South Asia and IOR. One can argue that it was due to India that China was able to pave its way into the Indian Ocean Region as New Delhi created an environment that was favourable for China and didn't step up its game to resist its foray into India's immediate neighbourhood. Thus Australia, Japan and the United States had begun to promote the term "Indo-Pacific" and especially the U.S. President Donald Trump had stressed on the importance of India, giving India an opportunity to play an increased role in the region. The term Indo-Pacific is also laying emphasis on the importance of the maritime domain, recently India and Australia acknowledged that "many of the future challenges are likely to occur in, and emanate from, the maritime domain underlining the re-emergence of the maritime space as the theatre for geopolitical competition". (Ministry of External Affairs, Media Center, 2020).

New Delhi was quite vague about its stance on the concept of the Indo-Pacific and was hesitant to be part of it initially and it struggled to explain the notion within its political framework as Australia,

Japan and the United States had done previously. Until the Shangri-La Dialogue of 2018, New Delhi decided to embrace the concept of "Indo-Pacific" as propounded by Prime Minister Narendra Modi. (Ministry of External Affairs, Media Center, 2018) Till Modi's speech at the Shangri-La Dialogue, Japan, the United States and Australia the proponents of the "Indo-Pacific" concept stressed on the importance of India and the strategic hedge that it holds and India carefully explored the costs and benefits in the region. India wanted to maintain an equilibrium as well as attain just the right balance between the United States and its allies and China on the other hand. And India didn't seek to partake in a policy of containment against China perpetuated by the Western powers, however at the same time India was in dire need of a new strategy given China's rise in its own backyard.

And soon India decided to follow the "Indo-Pacific" Strategy, along with other states India realized that it should play a greater role and acknowledged the need to balance the rising China in its immediate neighbourhood. (Medcalf, 2019) (Paul, 2018) However, India did not want to be seen as it is band wagoning with the West against a China centric order, and has repeatedly stated that it has no motive to contain China. However, India's participation in the Indo-Pacific strategy has a different meaning. Even though India is planning to play a greater role, its immediate focus will be on its neighbourhood where the threat from other forces is imminent. Meanwhile, China has been ramping up its presence in the South China Sea, a hotly contested area and is nearer to the Indian Ocean.

During the 2018, key note speech made by Prime Minister Narendra Modi at the Shangri-La Dialogue, he used the term "inclusive" four times, emphasising that the "Indo-Pacific envisaged by India must be a free, open, inclusive region—"FOIIP" rather than Japan's FOIP (Free and Open Indo-Pacific) and for New Delhi, the relations with Beijing is one of the top priorities and both sides are keen on maintaining a stable bilateral relationship" (Takenori, 2018). One point of contention between India and China in the Indo-Pacific would be on the definition of the rules-based order and the primary challenge would be China's resistance against the accepted rules and norms in the international order. Thus, the changes brought about in the current international order are mainly spearheaded (or as a consequence) of China. (Pant, 2016) In other words, China wants to go against an order that was created by the West and made for the West. Whereas India is in a tricky situation or in a state of dilemma, as it had no intention to partake in a policy of containment against China, even though it means that China's rise could undermine India's role around its region, hampering the security.

India's goals are clear, and it just wants to use the Indo-Pacific to move forward with its interests and does not wish to be seen as part of a coalition consisting of Western states against China. Given the changes brought by an aggressive China on the international order, it is natural that China will protest against the concept of the "Indo-Pacific" as a new geographic reality which is intended to undermine the unilateral actions taken by China. (Pant, 2016) Prior to the Shangri-La Dialogue of 2018, in January 2015, India and the United States agreed on the importance of the oceans surrounding it and issued a joint vision for the "Asia-Pacific and the Indian Ocean region." (The White House Office of the Press Secretary, 2015) It highlights the significance of the Indian Ocean, and proposed to separate it from the Asia-Pacific Theatre and it prioritized the respective region for each other, i.e., the Indian Ocean for India and the Asia-Pacific for the U.S. And shortly within a few months India entered into an agreement with Japan called the India-Japan Vision 2025, incorporating the region of Indian Ocean to the Indo-Pacific. (Ministry of External Affair, Media Centre, 2015) One should note that most of these developments have taken place in 2015 when the political scenario was different as compared to 2020. India's decision to side with Japan on the concept of Indo-Pacific was mainly due to the trust between both the countries and several other political factors (and its distinction between the Asia-Pacific and the Indian Ocean with Washington reflected otherwise.) However, in the coming years there was a change in stance from the U.S. especially since President Donald Trump was elected and both New Delhi and Washington began to closely work together on the Indo-Pacific strategy.

India is using its partnerships with other democratic states as the main point of contention for the Indo-Pacific Strategy. Modi's Shangri-La dialogue of 2018, confirmed India's definition of the Indo-Pacific as being "from the shores of Africa to that of the Americas." There are 4 key takeaways from Modi's speech, firstly, the strategy heavily relies on partnerships and collaborations, thus proving India's change in stance i.e., "its shift from isolation to active engagements with regards to its foreign policy". Secondly, India is strictly against an "alliance of containment" against China, this was a message for smaller countries who do not wish to be caught in between the Sino-Indian or Chinese-U.S. geopolitical rivalry (Ministry of External Affair, Media Centre,

2018). New Delhi wished to see itself as a nation who seeks to avoid any sort of confrontation between themselves and other great powers through cooperation and providing solutions in an era of great power competition. Thirdly, India acknowledges that there are alterations in the "global power" and these "foundations of the global order appear shaken." (Ministry of External Affair, Media Centre, 2018) Therefore, New Delhi is emphasizing on the principles of "free, open, and inclusive, with strong values and principles that respect to law, dialogues, rules, customs, and norms for the basis of a new order". Additionally, India promises to extend its support to other regional security architecture like ASEAN and to push for a multipolar world.

By 2020, India has a clear vision especially within the Indo-Pacific framework, the MEA stated that "Through the Indo-Pacific construct, India envisages a greater role for itself in the wider region." (Ministry of External Affairs: Annual Report, 2018). With partnerships from other countries like Australia, France, Japan, and the United States, India was able to expand its presence and these countries have emerged as India's natural partners. India has taken efforts to further expand their Indo-Pacific strategy well into the continent of Africa, Indonesia, Oman, and Singapore (and other organizations like ASEAN and the European Union). Initially India's initiatives in the Indo-Pacific were centred around the infrastructure collaborations with Japan. In 2015 Japan introduced its "Partnership for Quality Infrastructure" which is a direct dig against China's BRI. It promises sustainability, quality, feasible finance, and responsibility and termed China's BRI as a "cheap, but shoddy" alternative. ("Announcement of "Partnership for Quality Infrastructure: Investment for Asia's Future"", n.d.) (Prime Minister of Japan and His Cabinet, 2015)· The collaboration between India and Japan resulted in the Asia-Africa Growth Corridor, an initiative which is seen as a direct alternative to China's Maritime Silk Road.

The initiative proposed by India and Japan is based on the trust between these two states with an element of democracy (hinting at transparency). And both the countries are looking forward to providing better alternatives to nations in the Indian Ocean and Southeast Asia aimed at addressing the new security challenges in the region. ("India, Japan review situation in Indo-Pacific; resolve to ramp up cooperation in third countries", 2019) If Tokyo was the main economic partner for the regional states, then India too played a crucial role in assisting many nations in South Asia and the Indian Ocean by providing security. The initiatives include a port in "Chabahar (Iran), a terminal in Sri Lanka, possible infrastructure projects in Afghanistan, Bangladesh, Indonesia, Kenya and Vietnam". However, despite all these collaborations and efforts, India and Japan have struggled to transform much of these agreements into a reality, especially the Asia-Africa Growth Corridor which is yet to realize any projects. (Asia Africa Growth Corridor, 2017). There are several reasons for it, the main one being that India cannot match "Japan's expertise or capital in infrastructure development". One also needs to understand the fact that India's infrastructure collaborations with Japan was an immediate response to China's rising influence in the region.

The China Question- Potential partner in the Indo-Pacific?

The change that Beijing intended to bring about in the Indo-Pacific region is a direct threat to New Delhi's position as the main security provider and regional power. This can be partially attributed to India's negligence to its neighbours and its assertive and dominant nature left countries like Bangladesh, Maldives, Nepal, and Sri Lanka with no choice but to welcome China and gradually increase its presence. China is offering a better and lucrative alternative to these countries dwarfing India's offers and these countries are possibly looking forward to reducing its dependencies with India. With the advent of the Belt and Road Initiatives (BRI) China was able to offer even better infrastructure deals which these countries were lacking and gradually China was able to make inroads into India's neighbourhood. While New Delhi was carefully observing the rising Chinese wave in its neighbourhood, it was not until 2017 that India took a stance against the BRI project. (Ministry of External Affair: Media Centre, 2017)

India is concerned with the amount of debt that its neighbours owe to China due to the unsustainable projects. One such example would be the case of Hambantota Port in Sri Lanka, where Sri Lanka leased that port of China as part of debt-to-equity swap for a period of ninety-nine years. The Port is strategically important as it is really close to India's territorial waters and it has the potential to be used for military purposes thereby affecting the security of India, and Hambantota is just the tip of an iceberg. There are many other projects in the Indian Ocean Region that might fall under the Chinese control due to its unbefitting nature. Moreover, these islands are in "close proximity to key Sea Lanes of Communication (SLOCs) critical for the movement of goods and people in times of both peace and conflict" (Baruah, 2020). In other words, these islands are positioned in a way that they are near the main trading routes in the Indian Ocean, especially around the key choke points which could determine the naval presence across the region.

As a result of these developments, India took the opportunity to assess its relations with its neighbours and has taken note of their discontent and the absence of alternative strategic plans. Therefore, it led to an official prime ministerial visit from India to Mauritius, Seychelles, and Sri Lanka in 2015 and this is the first in two decades. Such a change in stance from India should be accredited to China, and India began to look more into its neighbouring states. Earlier India failed to properly address the issues faced by these nations and its proposals were believed to benefit just India, rather than creating a win-win situation for both the sides. However, New Delhi has a difficult task ahead in countering the Chinese wave and in its efforts to further reinvigorate its ties with these states.

Since India is looking forward to associate more with these island nations, it has made several changes in the Ministry of External Affairs (MEA) and established the Indian Ocean Region Division, "thus grouping the island states of Maldives, Mauritius, Seychelles, and Sri Lanka (later the small island nations of Madagascar, Comoros and the French territory of Reunion islands were added) together for the better coordination of initiatives and policy in the Indian Ocean." ("MEA Expands Indian Ocean Division to Include Islands off African Coast", 2019). Earlier, the states like Maldives and Sri Lanka were under the South Asian neighbourhood whereas Seychelles and Mauritius were under the Africa Division. The changes brought by India signify the importance of these small island nations and the maritime domain rather than grouping them into South Asia.

Multilateral Mechanisms and Related Policies

India is also interested in expanding its relationship with the European Union and vice-versa. They both have a common interest in "maintaining a rules-based order" in the Indo-Pacific and supporting regional organisations like the ASEAN and the IORA. In December 2018, Brussels signed an agreement with New Delhi acknowledging and adopting a strategy to "strengthen cooperation and partnership." (European Commission, 2018). This signifies that Europe wants to recognize India as an important player and is "supporting its bid to increase its own strategic profile in an evolving multipolar world". India being the founding member of the IORA, now a 22-member grouping, working to enhance sustainable development of an Indian Ocean blue economy.

V. Muraleedharan, the Minister of State for External Affairs of India, stated that "India attaches great preference to the IORA, and it is the most innovative, unique and broad-based platform for inter-regional partnership, connecting through the seas the world's most dynamic regions of South, South-East and West Asia, Oceania and Africa." The Indian trade and industry sectors have the capacity and the potential to contribute and enhance intra-IORA trade as well as encouraging tourism between the member states. India is the "largest contributor to the IORA Special Fund" and has taken active steps to support the bolstering of the IORA Secretariat by sharing expertise. ("Indian Ocean Rim Association discusses ways to achieve larger cooperation", 2019).

Due to the evolving nature of the Sino-Indian competition, the African continent has particularly gained prominence, especially on the west coast facing the Indian Ocean. However, India has been struggling to mark its presence as they expected it to be and they aim to renew old partnerships and establish new ones. In the maritime domain, the Indian Navy is taking measures to increase its area of influence, especially in the Western Indian Ocean by initiating capacity building and humanitarian assistance measures. The Western Indian Ocean is known for its crucial choke points from the "Mozambique Channel in the south to the Bab-el-Mandeb Strait in the North, the African continent could emerge as a playground for the great power competition". To signify the significance of the African continent, India has taken efforts to "send an official delegation and announced the opening of eighteen new missions in Africa to strengthen its political and strategic interests in the region". (Ministry of External Affair: Media Center: Press Release, 2018).

As stated earlier there has been a change in India's stance regarding the small island nations in the Indo-Pacific and it has begun to recognize the importance of such small islands. Earlier they were not considered that important and were long ignored. And the Indo-Pacific strategy provides an excellent stage for India to expand its collaborations, especially with the ones that are located near key choke points and the ones beyond the Indian Ocean. "New Delhi had hosted two summits of the Forum for India-Pacific Islands Cooperation (FIPC) in 2014, 2015 and India was supposed to host the 2020 edition". Moreover, New Delhi recently participated in the Pacific Islands Developing

States (PSIDS) and was "committed to provide $1 million to members of PSIDS for high-impact projects of their choice" ("Prime Minister meets Pacific Island Leaders", 2019). At the meeting, Prime Minister Narendra Modi stressed that India is "committed to advancing development priorities of Pacific Island Countries (PICs)". Additionally, India has also offered a line of credit of $150 million to the Pacific Island nations for projects involving solar power, and any other renewable energy sources, that are related to climate change.

In the past few years, there has been a steady positive shift in India's approach towards the PICs. Various geopolitical, economic and strategic factors could be possible reasons for this change. "Geo- strategically, the PICs are a part of the larger Indo-Pacific region. As the global focus shifts from Europe to the Indo-Pacific, the South Pacific sub-region lying at the crossroads of strategically significant maritime trade routes, comprising small island countries with large EEZs is also attracting attention from regional and extra-regional powers" (Pandey, 2020). India participates in the Pacific Island Forum (PIF) as one of the main dialogue partners and as stated above India has been engaged in the formation of FIPIC. Given the nature of the environment surrounding the Indo-Pacific, there are certain fields where even more cooperation can be established between India and PICs. The PICs can be attractive sources of natural resources like LNG (Liquefied Natural Gas) and hydrocarbons, given their resource rich EEZs. This could be beneficial to fuel India's developing economy and could also provide opportunities for a new market. Considering its own emphasis on the idea of "Blue Economy", India has the chance to better engage with these nations.

Another avenue of cooperation would be based on assistance and capacity building in disaster management. Most of the PICs are susceptible to natural disasters, India could assist in capacity building and establish better infrastructure to fight against such natural calamities. "In September 2017, India launched Climate Early Warning Systems in seven PICs. India has regularly provided assistance in these counties to deal with consequences of frequent cyclones like the relief and rehabilitation grant was provided when Tropical Cyclone Hola hit Vanuatu in 2018" (Pandey, 2020). Another area of confluence would be in terms of the medical and healthcare sector. Bearing in mind India's own expertise and abilities regarding the pharmaceutical industries, India aims to set up a pharmaceutical manufacturing pant, which would serve as a distribution centre in the Pacific Island region. This would enable the regional nations to gain a better access to affordable drugs and will provide India with an opportunity explore the healthcare sector of these countries. A line of credit for this project has also been offered in addition to India's willingness to provide necessary developmental and technical assistance required for capacity building measures.

Since Australia, Japan and the United States have become India's natural partners, New Delhi hosts annual 2+2 Dialogues with them (it also includes France as well). Moreover, there are numerous annual meets on issues ranging from cybersecurity, counterterrorism, science and technology and space. Recently India concluded the 2+2 dialogue with the United States. The U.S. sent its Secretary of State, Mike Pompeo and Defence Secretary, Mark T. Esper and they were met by their Indian counterparts and Prime Minister Narendra Modi. "The main outcome of the meeting was the signing of the Indo-US Basic Exchange and Cooperation Agreement for geo-spatial coordination". This would provide access to the "highly accurate navigation satellite networks" run by the US. (Venkataramakrishnan, 2020).

New Delhi is also looking forward to tackling non-traditional security threats and promoting sustainable developments as well as promoting "blue economy and ocean development". Such initiatives could hugely benefit the small island nations in the Indo-Pacific. Furthermore, there are Quadrilateral (or Quad) meetings between India, Japan, Australia and the United States beginning from 2019. (Panda, 2019). As a result of their close ties and the evolving nature of their relationship, the Ministry of Defence declared that Australia will participate in the 2020 edition of the Malabar naval exercise. "As India seeks to increase cooperation with other countries in the maritime security domain and in the light of increased defence cooperation with Australia, Malabar, 2020 will see the participation of the Australian Navy," the Ministry said in a statement. (Peri, 2020).

With these collaborations, India hopes to "coordinate and address common challenges and threats, providing a platform to offer solutions and initiatives and presenting itself in a leadership role", as a result it would boost India's credibility in the international sphere towards its role as a world leader in a multipolar world. In spite of India's global outreach and commitments, New Delhi's immediate goal revolves around the Indian Ocean. Any sort of structural and fundamental changes in the region would have a direct impact on India's security. It is a known fact that, at times of emergency India would focus all its resources on securing the Indian Ocean. Given the changing dynamics of the Indian Ocean, there is a need to alter India's military and security response.

6 Multilateral and Plurilateral Talks

India-Maldives-Sri Lanka Trilateral Maritime Security Cooperation Initiative

In October 2011, the Trilateral Maritime Security Co-operation Initiative was instituted by India, Maldives and Sri Lanka. Following the first NSA-level Trilateral Meeting, two subsequent meetings took place in 2013 and 2014 respectively. Undertaken just a few days after the Chinese takeover of the Gwadar port, the trilateral initiative saw substantive advancements in the second NSA-level meeting where the three sides agreed to enhance collaborations in the "Maritime Domain Awareness (MDA)" with the provision of Long Range Identification and Tracking (LRIT) services to Sri Lanka and the Maldives, MDA training in India, coordination in Search and Rescue (SAR) operations and communication on illegal maritime activities as well as sharing of "Merchant Ship Information System (MSIS) software by India and Automatic Identification System (AIS) data" on a trilateral format. (Ministry of External Affair, Media Center: Bilateral/ Multilateral Documents, 2013). The three littoral countries also agreed to strengthen bilateral 'DOSTI' exercises. Notably, the India-Maldives 'DOSTI' exercises were expanded to include Sri Lanka for a trilateral Joint-Coast Guard exercise off the coast of Male in 2012.

Progress made on these activities was reviewed in the third NSA-level meeting which took place in March 2014 in New Delhi and laid the roadmap for "new areas of cooperation including hydrography; training in Visit, Board, Search and Seizure Operations; training on-board Indian Sail Training Ships; exchanges between think tanks;

and joint participation in adventure activities." (Ministry of External Affair: Public Diplomacy, 2014). The meeting also saw participation from Mauritius and Seychelles as guest countries. The possible expansion of the initiative in its current form is to include other nations in the region under its ambit is something that has seen particular interest from India. This was reiterated by Prime Minister Narendra Modi in March 2015 during his visit to the Indian Ocean Islands where in laying a five-fold framework for Indian maritime engagements in the Indian Ocean region, he expressed support for the inclusion of Mauritius and Seychelles in the current initiative. (Mohan, 2015). However, the group lacks clarity on the issue. For instance, while India has expressed open support for the inclusion of Mauritius, Sri Lanka has often expressed its frustration with the latter over its backing of a UN Human Rights resolution critical of its actions. ("Sri Lanka upset with Mauritius over rights resolution", 2014). The inclusion of Mauritius and Seychelles in the next NSA-level security dialogue is a question that still looms in the dark since the initiative has not seen another meeting in over five years. This is in part due to political turmoil in the Maldives where the fourth meeting was to take place. New Delhi's dissatisfaction with the Maldives' Yameen government was a clear setback for the maritime initiative. Political differences of this nature and other issues like the fishermen dispute between India and Sri Lanka are contentious matters which hold the potential to impede progress in security collaboration on the maritime frontier. Resolution of these differences and further convergence of interests is imperative for cohesive maritime cooperation under the trilateral initiative.

India-Australia-France Trilateral Dialogue

The requisite for instituting a trilateral partnership which builds on the existing synergies amongst India, Australia and France is a notion which has been circulated widely in policy circles. The notion was reiterated by French President, Emmanuel Macron during his visit to Australia in 2018 where he advocated for "a new Paris-Delhi-Canberra axis as a key for the region with joint objectives in the Indian-Pacific region", while calling for better organization of like-minded actors to counter aggression in the Indo-Pacific. ("Macron wants strategic Paris-Delhi-Canberra axis amid Pacific tension", 2018). Resonating the same essence, on the 9th September, 2020, the first India-France-Australia Trilateral Dialogue at the senior official level was conducted virtually.

The trilateral dialogue, which the three nations have agreed to hold annually ahead, was centred around the need to enhance cooperation in the Indo-Pacific region. The dialogue follows what has often been described as France's emerging pivot to the Indo-Pacific.

The French Ministry for the Armed Forces' 2019 policy document, *"France and Security in the Indo-Pacific"*, outlines France's stakes in the region, drawing attention to the 9 million square kms of Exclusive Economic Zone and the 7,000 military personnel-strong presence that the country holds there. (Ministry of Armed Forces of France, 2019). What then draws the three countries together is their shared interest in upholding a free and open Indo-Pacific and their common democratic values. Notably, the Trilateral Dialogue, which was organized while India and China engaged in a standoff at the Line of Actual Control (LAC) in Ladakh, follows the change in dynamics of the relationship that the three nations share with China. Given that the key focus area of the Dialogue is centred around the maintenance of stability in the Indo-Pacific security complex, it comes as no surprise that the central area of cooperation under the partnership is that of combined maritime effort. The meeting, which discussed both geostrategic and economic challenges in the Indo-Pacific in the context of the COVID-19 pandemic, laid particular emphasis on cooperation in the Global Marine Commons. The three countries intend to undertake this at both a trilateral and regional level. Considering the multilateral networks that India, Australia and France hold, drawing upon their compatibility is crucial for the three to enhance their partnership. It is in this light that the Trilateral Dialogue emphasized the need to utilize regional platforms like the, Indian Ocean Commission, ASEAN and IORA to enhance practical cooperation.

India's Policies towards the Korean Peninsula, South China Sea and East China Sea

- ***India-Japan-Australia Trilateral Dialogue***
  The first India-Japan-Australia Trilateral Dialogue was held in June of 2015 in New Delhi with closer security and economic ties on the agenda. The clear focus of the first meeting of the dialogue was maritime security in the South China Sea. Indicating the will to strengthen military cooperation, the three signalled the possibility of joint naval exercises. It must be noted the three states

are core members of the Quadrilateral Security Dialogue along with the United States as well. India's decision to invite Australia to join the 2020 Malabar exercises which will also see participation from Japan and the U.S. is indicative of growing concert between their naval forces. However, the India-Japan-Australia Trilateral Dialogue is unique on two fronts: First, it is a forum of three medium powers of the Indo-Pacific, each with an ability to influence regional stability significantly and each without any historical grievances with the other. (Joshi, 2017). The arrangement also does not include the United States and therefore, in the face of uncertain and waning U.S. security leadership, can retain a stable front. Regardless, the present structure of the arrangement supports American presence in the region's security complex. Second, the geographical geometry of the India-Japan-Australia triangle is highly significant for the Indo-Pacific arc. Prominence of security cooperation in the meeting agendas thereby follows naturally. The first three meetings under the Trilateral Dialogue concentrated on enhancing naval cooperation and disaster relief operations. The fourth meeting of the three nations expanded the agenda to include discussions on North Korea, territorial disputes in Southeast Asia as well as seaborne terror. However, realizing the full potential of the Trilateral will require a stronger emphasis on regional infrastructure building and stronger bilateral ties, upon which the arrangement ultimately rests.

- ***India and the Korean Peninsula***

  India's Policy Towards North Korea and South Korea

  The relationship between India and North Korea, which finds its origins in the Cold War period when both nations relied on Soviet armaments, is one of consistent but very subdued nature. Despite Western scepticism, India has maintained its diplomatic presence in Pyongyang and provided the country with food and medical aid in face of its shortages over the years. In May 2018, General V.K. Singh the then Minister of State for External Affairs of India, visited North Korea after a gap of almost twenty years and the two countries agreed to strengthen cultural and educational cooperation. (Ministry of External Affairs, Media Center: Press Release, 2018). A few months later, the Indian delegation to the ASEAN Regional Forum had a second meeting with the DPRK's Foreign Minister, Ri Yong Ho. New Delhi also provided training for DPRK officials "under the Indian Technical and Economic Cooperation Program (ITEC) and its Professional Course for Foreign Diplomats (PCFD)". These training efforts, however, have been stranded since 2016 in response to the UNSC Resolution 2270 which was adopted after North Korea carried out a fourth nuclear test and launched another satellite. (Pubby & Chaudhury, 2018). India has taken a strong stance on the significance of North Korea's denuclearization process. In 2017, New Delhi imposed strict sanctions on North Korea and halted its trade relations with the country. (Ministry of External Affairs, 2017) Recognizing North Korea's nuclear tests as a security threat (Chatterji, 2017) and participating in the Vancouver Dialogue on North Korea opens more options for India to reinforce its standing in the Indo-Pacific geopolitical calculus. Another clear focus in India's stance in this regard is its concern over defence technology cooperation and nuclear commerce between North Korea and Pakistan. While playing the role of an intermediary for the Korea issue would be too far-fetched for India, its engagements in the Peninsula are not passive altogether. India chaired the nine-member UN Commission that overlooked Korean elections in 1947 and is one of the only 25 countries with an embassy in Pyongyang. The country's distinct position on the Korean Peninsula and the increase in its Indo-Pacific engagements may allow it to play a constructive role on the matter in the future (Panda, 2020).

However, India's relations with South Korea, which were formally established in 1962, have gained significant momentum in recent years. This recent uptick in bilateral relations is largely a result of the resonance between the South Korean President, Moon Jae-in's recent "New Southern Policy" (NSP) and India's "Act East policy". The common strand between the two policies is that of expanding economic engagement in South and Southeast Asia. Nonetheless, there is a strategic streak that runs through these policies as well. In May 2015, the two countries upgraded the status of their bilateral relations to that of a "Special Strategic Partnership" and agreed to establish a 2+2 consultation mechanism in their 'Joint Statement for Special Strategic Partnership'. The Indian and South Korean Coast Guards signed a Memorandum of Understanding in 2005 and have conducted multiple joint exercises since. Another area of cooperation is that of the defence industry. In September 2019, the two countries signed an agreement to expand naval logistical support towards each other, an arrangement that India had hitherto shared with only the United States and France. (Rajagopalan, 2019). Bilateral relations between India and South Korea, however, are complicated by their relations with other regional actors. South Korea, which is economically dependent on China, has exhibited reluctance on taking a stronger stance on Sino-Indian disputes.

At the same time, India has exhibited a similar reluctance in explicitly siding with a party in the Dokdo/Takeshima dispute between South Korea and Japan. Regardless, the policy orientations of the two countries are largely compatible. Both India and South Korea share common apprehensions about nuclear relations between North Korea and Pakistan and increasing Chinese assertiveness. India's support for the denuclearization process and peaceful Inter-Korean engagement has also been well received by South Korea. Notably, while South Korea has not openly adopted the Indo-Pacific framework, its policies clearly lend support for a free and open Indo-Pacific.

- ***India and the South China Sea***

India's interest in the South China Sea rests on its economic security, its stakes in the regional stability of its extended neighbourhood and its obligations as a maritime power to lend support to the freedom of navigation in the region. The threat over freedom of navigation creates the central pillar in India's policy towards the South China Sea. Indian delegates to several ASEAN-centric forums have reiterated the need to uphold it in accordance with UNCLOS. The theme reappeared in its joint statement with the United States in October 2020 during the third India-U.S. 2+2 Ministerial Dialogue which specified that "the Code of Conduct in the South China Sea should not prejudice the legitimate rights and interests of any nation in accordance with international law". (Ministry of External Affairs, Media Center: Bilateral/Multilateral Documents, 2020). This becomes especially relevant for India since over 30 percent of its trade passes through the South China Sea ("How Much Trade Transits the South China Sea? | ChinaPower Project", 2017).

A qualitative shift in India's relations with Southeast Asian states has been underway since the launch of its 'Act East Policy' which expanded its scope to include both economic and security integration as compared to the earlier 'Look East Policy' which rested on an almost entirely economic underlining. Indo-Vietnamese oil cooperation between ONGC Videsh and Petro Vietnam corroborates both these aspects. In decisions aimed at sustaining Indian strategic and economic interests in the region, Vietnamese authorities have repeatedly renewed OVL's contract of oil exploration in Block-128, an oil block situated in contested waters of the South China Sea, despite strong Chinese opposition. The two countries conducted bilateral drills off the Cam Ranh Bay in April 2019. India marked its naval presence in the South China Sea in early 2000 and has frequently undertaken joint military exercises with ASEAN nations since. These include Singapore-India Maritime Bilateral Exercises (SIMBEX), MILAN exercises, the Indo-Thai Coordinated Patrol as well as the India-Indonesia Coordinated Patrol.

It must, however, be kept in mind that the main operation thrust of the Indian Navy remains in the Indian Ocean Region and in countering Chinese influence in its immediate neighbourhood first. While Indian authorities acknowledge certain apprehensions over Chinese assertiveness in the South China Sea, they nonetheless maintain a neutral stance of non-intervention and non-confrontation, given that the country is not party to maritime territorial disputes of Southeast Asia. (Singh, 2019). Besides, while India shares some of its concerns with the US regarding the South China Sea, it disagrees with the U.S. interpretation of maritime law to undertake innocent passage through a nation's Exclusive Economic Zone (EEZ) without prior notification or approval, understanding its security consequences for the Andaman and Nicobar Islands. India's stance on the South China Sea is, therefore, that of a security maximizer rather than a power maximizer, seeking to support its partners in the region while also maintaining its position on non-intervention.

- ***India-ASEAN Strategic Cooperation***

  The significance of India's position as security player in Southeast Asia has increased as a result of the complex security landscape in the region which induced Southeast Asian nations to open up strategic space for greater defence engagement with India and recognize its role in promoting regional stability. While India has been engaged with ASEAN countries both bilaterally and multilaterally since the inception of its 'Look East' policy in 1992, the central dynamics of this policy have been economic in nature. The policy, however, also acquired a strategic orientation with its transformation to the 'Act East' policy which is more proactive in its outlook.

Consistent with this policy is India's active participation in the ASEAN Regional Forum (ARF), which it joined in 1996, and in the ASEAN Defence Ministers' Meetings (ADMM)- Plus (Sajjanhar, 2018). Yet India's security engagement with the ASEAN countries still largely takes place at the bilateral level. Of these, one of the most significant partners for India is Singapore with which it shares a Comprehensive Defence Cooperation Agreement as well as a Bilateral Agreement for the Conduct of Joint Military Training and Exercises in India ("India Military Bilateral and Multilateral Exercises in 2019- A Compendium, 2019). The two navies have conducted joint SIMBEX exercises annually since 1994 and were allowed access to each other's bases in November 2017 with the finalization of the India-Singapore Bilateral Agreement for Navy Cooperation. (Parameswaran, 2017).

Private firms based in Singapore are also engaged in the production of defence systems and can provide a pathway for greater cooperation in defence technology between the two nations. India also shares a robust defence relationship with Vietnam which is key for its presence in Southeast Asia. After formalizing security cooperation in 2000, the two countries signed a Strategic Partnership Agreement in July 2007 aimed at enhancing regional security as well as civil nuclear and counter-terrorism cooperation. A central tenet of the India-Vietnam security relationship is that of capacity building. This was reiterated in the "Joint Vision Statement on Defence Cooperation for the period 2015-2020" that the two released in May 2015. (Ministry of External Affairs: Media Center, 2018). India has also extended a USD 500 million defence line of credit to Vietnam in addition to the USD 100 million line of credit that it provided for the development of patrol vessels for the Vietnamese Border Guards.

India's defence relations with Myanmar, Indonesia and Thailand are propelled by the high priority it accords to the maintenance of stability in its immediate neighbourhood. Given their proximity to the Andaman and Nicobar Islands, creating common perceptions regarding regional security and realizing the same through joint operations and initiatives becomes imperative. India regularly conducts Coordinated Patrol (CORPAT) exercises in the Indian Ocean Region with all three countries. Although India's CORPAT exercises with Indonesia were largely limited to tackling trafficking and other sea-borne illegal activities, the two nations have gradually expanded the ambit of their naval cooperation. (Ram, 2018). Following the MILAN exercise of 2014, both navies agreed to carry out IND-INDO Bilateral Naval Exercise in 2015. Indonesia was one of the first and strongest proponents in the ASEAN for the adoption of the Indo-Pacific outlook which resonated with India. "This shared vision on maritime cooperation in the Indo-Pacific is one of the central tenets of the Comprehensive Strategic Partnership that the two signed in May 2018". India's security relationship with Thailand and Myanmar, however, have developed at a relatively slower pace. In accordance with its vision for Security and Growth for All in the Region (SAGAR), India delivered INS Sindhuvir to Myanmar in October 2020 which marked the induction of the first submarine for Myanmar. This was a significant development in the defence relationship that Myanmar shares with India. However, while India has been expanding its security ties with Myanmar as well as other nations like the Philippines and Malaysia, these partnerships remain more symbolic in nature and lack substantive collaborative effort.

7 India's Economic Engagements in the Indo-Pacific

India's Trade Relations and key FTAs (Free Trade Agreements) in the Indo-Pacific

• ***ASEAN***

Trade and economic cooperation form a key aspect of India's engagement with ASEAN. The "Look East" policy was initiated in 1992 to establish and improve economic and strategic relations between South-East Asia and India. India-ASEAN relations expanded significantly and gained momentum under the ASEAN-India Comprehensive Economic Cooperation signed in 2009. The Agreement comprises of FTAs on goods as well as services and investment between India and ASEAN. India-ASEAN relations have strengthened with the shift from the 'Look East' to the 'Act East' policy.

Signed in 2009, the ASEAN-India Free Trade Agreement (AIFTA) came into effect in 2010. Under AIFTA, members of ASEAN and India agreed to steadily eliminate tariffs on 80 percent of the tariff lines, accounting for 75 percent of the trade. Prior to the signing of the AIFTA, India's total trade with ASEAN was valued at USD 42 billion in 2009 with merchandise imports accounting for USD 24 billion and

[1] Around 489 tariff lines (HS6 Digit level) have been excluded from tariff concessions and 590 tariff lines from the list of tariff elimination by India to protect interests of sectors and industries such as agriculture, textiles, auto, petrochemicals, etc. ASEAN countries have also put forward country wise exclusion lists.

merchandise exports accounting for USD 42 billion. According to a study conducted by, following the AIFTA, India's total merchandise trade increased from USD 53 billion in 2010 to USD 93 billion in 2018 with merchandise exports increasing from USD 23 billion to USD 36 billion and merchandise imports increasing from USD 30 billion to USD 57 billion for the same period. (Bhogal, 2018)

The ASEAN-India Agreement on Services and Investments was signed in 2015. India's total trade in services with ASEAN for 2018-19 amounted to USD 45 billion with exports accounting for USD 24 billion and imports accounting for USD 21 billion. India received around USD 13.8 billion as FDI from ASEAN countries during 2015-16. Singapore is a primary hub for FDI inflows and outflows to and from India. It accounts for more than 99 percent of total FDI inflows into India, with the rest ASEAN countries contributing to less than 1 percent. India's FDI outflows to ASEAN valued at USD 1.2 billion in 2015 accounted for 1.3 percent of total net inflows into ASEAN (Bhogal, 2018).

Besides pursuing economic partnership at a regional level, India has signed bilateral agreements with ASEAN members such as Singapore, Thailand, and Malaysia to promote economic integration. The India-Singapore Comprehensive Economic Cooperation Agreement has contributed to the significant expansion of economic and trade relations.

Following the AIFTA, India's imports from ASEAN increased by 79 percent while the exports increased by 39 percent. India's trade deficit with ASEAN has widened significantly and currently amounts to USD 24 billion. This can be attributed to a variety of factors, ranging from poor competitiveness of the Indian manufacturing sector and underutilization of opportunities provided by regional and bilateral FTAs owing to limited knowledge among Indian exporters, presence of non-tariff trade barriers and exploitation of FTA and lenient rules of origin by routing products from third countries to India through the India-ASEAN and India-Singapore FTA. India is seeking to review its FTA with ASEAN due to concerns of the widening deficit and underutilization of certain lines. India and ASEAN are currently conducting scoping exercises to determine the scope of the review. (Mitra & Srivas, 2020)

India has also undertaken projects to improve connectivity and enhance integration between India and South-East Asia. Improved infrastructure and transportation facilities within India as well as between India and South-east Asia, particularly Myanmar through the North East and maritime links is key to greater integration between Indian and South-east Asian markets. India has undertaken the Kaladan Multi-Modal Transport project, India-Myanmar-Thailand Trilateral Highway, and the Rih Tedim Project in Myanmar to improve connectivity between India and South-East Asia (Seshadri, 2014). The Rih-Tedim project aims to establish connectivity between eastern Mizoram and western Mizoram. The Kaladan Multi-Modal Transit Transport Project will connect Kolkata port with Sittwe in Myanmar, Myanmar with Mizoram by road. The India-Myanmar-Thailand (IMT) Trilateral Highway, once completed, will connect Moreh, India with Mae Sot in Thailand via Myanmar and will enhance trade in the ASEAN-India Free Trade Area. India is interested in extending the highway to Cambodia, Laos, and Vietnam through, what will be known as, the East-West Economic Corridor (EWEC). (Bhogal, 2018)

- ***Australia***

Trade between India and Australia has increased from USD 9.3 billion in 2007 to USD 20.8 billion in 2018. While trade between the two countries has grown steadily, it remains skewed towards Australia. For instance, India imports from Australia accounted for USD 13.3 billion whereas Australia's imports from India accounted for USD 3.52 billion, leading to a trade deficit of around USD 10 billion. However, the deficit is a result of India's dependence on Australia for coal. India and Australia began negotiations on the Australia-India Comprehensive Economic Agreement in 2011 but talks came to a standstill in 2015 due to their involvement in RCEP (Regional Comprehensive Economic Partnership). During its bilateral negotiations, India was concerned about the treatment of agriculture in the agreement and the impact of Australian agricultural products on its domestic sector.

Another issue of disagreement between India and Australia has been regarding the inclusion of the dairy sector in the trade deal. Since its withdrawal from the RCEP, India has shown interest in signing a bilateral agreement with RCEP member countries. While Australia has highlighted the need for India to reconsider its decision of withdrawal from RCEP, it has expressed its interest in expanding economic cooperation through an agreement as it remains keen on reducing dependence on China due to concerns about increasing Chinese interference in its domestic politics, South Pacific, and the South China Sea. In a Joint Ministerial Commission held in 2020, the countries agreed to discuss issues of harmonizing standards and regulatory barriers.

In July 2020, during the Indo-Australia summit, India and Australia elevated their relations from that of a Strategic Partnership to a level of Comprehensive Strategic Partnership. The two countries discussed the need to proceed with negotiations on a trade deal. In addition, an agreement on mining and the processing of strategic minerals was concluded. This will help augment the 'Make in India' programme, particularly the automobile and electric car industry. While India and Australia have strengthened their strategic relations and remain keen on expanding their trade and economic relations, any future trade agreement between India and Australia is likely to remain contingent on the treatment and inclusion of agriculture and the dairy sector as well as rules concerning the movement of individuals (mode IV in the GATS).

- ***New Zealand***

As of 2020, New Zealand's bilateral exports to India accounted for nearly USD 1.06 billion while its bilateral imports from India amounted to USD 650 billion. While tourism contributed a major share of New Zealand's exports to India of nearly 60 percent of the total exports, India's exports to New Zealand consisted of goods.

New Zealand and India have been negotiating a bilateral trade agreement, officially titled as the Comprehensive Economic Cooperation Agreement (CECA), since 2010. The CECA was expected to cover trade in goods, services, and investment. While India has successfully signed such pacts with countries such as Singapore, South Korea, Japan and Malaysia, the economic cooperation agreement with New Zealand proved to be elusive so far. One of the key obstacles in the finalization of the CECA with New Zealand is in relation to its fear of agricultural and dairy imports from New Zealand flooding its markets and harming its domestic sectors. (Sen, 2017)

There remains a large scope for New Zealand and India to promote trade in several sectors of mutual interest. India could benefit from New Zealand's expertise in the food processing industry, cold storage chains and the dairy sector whereas New Zealand could benefit from India's expertise in industries such as pharmaceuticals and the information technology services. While this may require India to open selected sectors of the agriculture and dairy which is an extremely sensitive issue, on New Zealand's part they may have to do more to adopt more liberal policies in relation to immigration, which has been one of India's concerns.

- ***Pacific Island Nations***

The fourteen countries located in the South-West Pacific Ocean (Pacific Island countries or PICs) are islands with low levels of population. These are, however, strategically, and economically important due to their Exclusive Economic Zones (EEZ) which are rich in natural but also mineral resources such as Liquefied Natural gas (LNG), hydrocarbons. For example, Kiribati, a small PIC has an EEZ of 3.5 Million Square Kilometers.

Despite having a large Indian diaspora ("nearly 40 percent of Fiji's population is of Indian origin"), until recently, India's engagement with PICs has been limited. Even this limited engagement was confined to countries such as Fiji to the neglect of the other PICs. In contrast, countries such as Australia, New Zealand, the US and, of late, China have provided significant amounts of aid to PICs that are aid-dependent. With India's strategic interests expanding in the Indo-Pacific region, India is increasingly engaging with the South Pacific region emphasizing on its willingness to strengthen relations, particularly in the context of its 'Act East' policy. (Pandey, 2020)

In 2014, PM Modi visited Fiji (the first by an Indian Prime Minister in 33 years) and launched the Forum for India-Pacific Island Cooperation (FIPIC) that serves to promote multi-dimensional cooperation at a multilateral level. In 2014, India announced a Special Adaptation Fund of USD 1 million to address climate change through technical assistance and capacity building. Rather than limiting its engagement to aid, India is undertaking efforts to improve trade relations with the PICs while looking to promote Indian investment in these countries. A 'Business accelerator' for FIPIC was set up in 2015 to facilitate trade and investment. (Wadhwa, 2019)

As of 2018, India's annual trade with PICs stands at around USD 300 million. However, India's trade with the region is confined to countries such as Fiji, Solomon Islands and Papua New Guinea. In 2016, an MOU was signed for a line of credit of USD 100 million for improvement of infrastructure in Papua New Guinea (PNG). India is engaged in several initiatives for improving the technological capabilities in Fijian industries such as sugar production, coconut-based industries etc. India has also initiated efforts in PICs to address issues such as climate change and improve the capacity of the local healthcare sector, etc. In 2019, India announced a grant of USD 12 million to PCIs for the implementation of development projects in sectors of their choice, in addition to a concessional line of credit of USD 150 million that was offered to countries for implementing renewable energy and climate-related projects depending on their requirements. At the upcoming 3rd FIPIC summit, India and PICs will undertake efforts to strengthen their cooperation on key issues such as trade and investment, blue economy, maritime security, sustainable development at the 3rd FIPIC summit. (Pandey, 2020).

India's Key Free Trade Agreements

- ***South Korea and India***

South Korea and India signed the Comprehensive Economic Partnership Agreement (CEPA) which became operational in 2010. The CEPA commits both the countries to lowering or phasing out of import tariffs on a wide range of goods covering nearly 85 to 90 percent of the bilateral trade. However, agricultural products and textiles have been excluded from tariff reforms considering they are sensitive sectors. Since the execution of the CEPA, the trade and economic ties between the two countries made great strides crossing the USD 20 billion mark during the year 2018. (Mukhopadhyay, 2020)

Korea's investment in India crossed the USD 1 billion mark during the 2018 with Korea's total FDI to India up to September 2019 amounting to USD 6.29 billion. Investments from India to Korea amounted to nearly USD 3 billion. Korea is an export-driven economy which besides having the world's largest shipbuilding is a major player in the production of semiconductors, electronic products, and automobiles. The CEPA covers services and allows up to 160 Indian professionals to access the Korean market on a temporary basis. (Mukhopadhyay, 2020).

India is currently exploring diversification of India's exports which are driven by petrochemical products, Naphtha, accounting for more than half of its exports to Korea. Both countries are exploring commercial opportunities in areas such as nuclear energy, space, and defence production.

Following the visit of Prime Minister Narendra Modi to Korea during 2015, it was decided that the India-Korea CEPA would be reviewed for an up-gradation. Since then, many meetings both at the ministerial level and officer levels have been held between both the nations. During a meeting between the trade ministers of both the countries in 2017, it was decided that a Joint Future Strategy Group would be established to identify opportunities for high-end technological cooperation. (Rai, 2019)

- ***Indo-Singapore Free Trade Agreement_***

India and Singapore had signed the Comprehensive Economic Cooperation Agreement (CECA) in the year 2005. The CECA covers trade in goods, services and investment. The CECA aimed to increase trade and investment bilaterally and facilitate the usage of Singapore as a gateway to increased trade with the broader South-East Asian and the Asia Pacific regions. The CECA also sought to "identify opportunities for Singapore companies to participate in Public-Private partnership projects in India and the possibilities of using Singapore as a base to raise infrastructure funding" (Seshadri, 2017). Increased cooperation in the areas of tourism, science and technology, media, intellectual property rights were other salient features of the CECA. The CECA aimed at a tariff reduction on nearly 82 percent of Singapore's exports to India. Singapore, in any case, is permitted to trade with no or minimal tariffs even without a CECA. Singapore and India were also part of India- ASEAN FTA signed in the year 2009. (Seshadri, 2017)

Following the CECA, India became the 12th biggest trading partner of Singapore in terms of exports for the FY 2015 (as compared to 15th in the year 2004) and 13th largest trading partner of Singapore in terms of its imports from India (as compared to 20th in the year 2004). In terms of trade volumes, the annual bilateral trade, between the two countries more than doubled from a mere USD 7 billion to USD 16 billion in 2015 (Seshadri, 2017).

Trade in services is another significant component of the CECA with the two countries committing to significant market openings. Following the CECA, three Singaporean banks- DBS, OCBC and UOB were permitted to open up to 15 branches in India. Singapore on the other hand permitted Indian banks to apply for full banking licenses with three Indian banks to be granted Qualified Full Banking (QFB) privileges which allow them to gain additional privileges. The CECA also granted relaxation to the two sovereign wealth funds- TEMASEK and GIC- to invest more in India by way of portfolio investment. (Seshadri, 2017)

- ***India-Japan Free Trade Agreement_***

India and Japan entered into a Comprehensive Economic Partnership Agreement (CEPA) in the year 2011 which aimed at phasing out of the tariffs on 90 percent of Japanese exports to India, and 97 percent of imports from India, including agricultural and fisheries products. The CECA also sought to address some of the key infrastructural constraints in India, generally seen as a hindrance to increased trade prospects. One of the key projects envisaged in this regard is the development of the Delhi–Mumbai Industrial Corridor (DMIC) project with an investment of nearly USD 90 billion involving the development of industrial zones; a high-speed freight line; ports; airports; expressway; and a 4,000-megawatt power plant. It is also expected that several non-tariff barriers in Japan that hinder prospects of trade would be removed particularly in areas such as pharmaceutical products where India has built up expertise and capacity in the generic medicines market. (Nataraj, 2014)

Despite the CEPA in force for nearly ten years now the India-Japan bilateral trade has not reached its full potential. For example, India's trade with Japan in 2018 amounted to USD 17.6 billion in 2018 which is just about 20 percent of its trade with China and is less than its trade with Korea. A case in point is India's pharmaceutical exports which stood a whopping USD 5.4 billion in 2018 as compared to a mere USD 60 million to Japan. India is now in discussions with Japan to review the CEPA to further increase the prospects for trade and investment flows between the two countries. (Rai, 2019)

Most of these free trade agreements are in need of a review to make it in sync with Fourth Industrial Revolution and expand the horizons of cooperation in digital, E commerce and promote regional production chains.

However, in the midst of India's associations with these nations on both economic and political fronts as well as collaborations with respect to the Indo-Pacific strategy, it is essential to take a look and evaluate India's Missed opportunities.

Missed Opportunities?

- ***Regional Comprehensive Economic Partnership (RCEP)***

The RCEP involves 10 countries from the ASEAN and its leading trade partners: Japan, South Korea, New Zealand, Australia, and China. The participating countries account for around one-third of the world's gross domestic product. India withdrew from the RCEP in 2019 after participating in negotiations for seven years. India's participation in the RCEP would have strengthened its geostrategic engagements with its partners in the Indo-Pacific, augmented its 'Act East' policy and integrated it with the region's supply chain networks. It would have also provided Indian exporters greater access to markets by reducing the trade costs and harmonizing trade rules.

India was justified in withdrawing from the RCEP. Its decision to withdraw was rooted in concerns that the RCEP did not address its concerns regarding safeguards against imports, non-tariff barriers vis-à-vis ASEAN and China, and rules of origin adequately. India's partners had supposedly insisted India accord them concessions it was granted to them, on an MFN (Most Favoured Nation) basis. India's decision must be analysed in context of China's participation in and perception of the RCEP as a hedge against the negative effects of the US-China trade war. Given the poor competitiveness of Indian industries, being a party to the RCEP would have only made it easier for China to dump its products on India, worsened India's ever-rising deficit and negatively affected its domestic industries. India was also concerned about dairy products from Australia and New Zealand affecting its domestic dairy sector. India's reluctance to participate in the RCEP was based on the fact that other countries were not very keen on accommodating India's interests in the services sector, particularly mode IV. (Kumar, 2019)

While there is no doubt that the RCEP would have served against India's national interests, particularly in the current geopolitical order, India's withdrawal also indicates its unpreparedness in participating in the current international trading environment. To address this, India must initiate serious efforts to strengthen its manufacturing sector, that enjoys protection and is far from competitive.

- ***Trans-Pacific Partnership***

The Trans-Pacific Partnership (TPP) signed by the United States and 11 other Pacific-Rim countries, namely Japan, Singapore, Brunei, Australia, Malaysia, Vietnam, New Zealand, Canada, Chile, Mexico and Peru, was no doubt devised to counter China's economic influence. India, through its Foreign Trade Policy 2020-25, made it evident that it would not be a part of the agreement.

If India were a party to the TPP, it would have had to conform and grant tariff concessions as required by the TPP. This would have eroded the Indian manufacturing sector which enjoys protection and is far from being competitive. The TPP also requires contracting countries to reduce or eliminate tariffs in the agricultural sector. Agriculture is an overly sensitive issue in India, as fears such concessions would flood Indian markets with cheap and subsidized products from the US, Australia, and New Zealand. The TPP raises the standards concerning IPR, beyond TRIPS (Trade Related Aspects of Intellectual

Property Rights) provisions and incorporates TRIPS-plus provisions into its regime. This would lead to the ever greening of drugs, extend the monopolies of pharmaceutical companies and reduce access and availability of generic drugs. (Chatterjee, 2016)

India would have had to conform to regulations on government procurement under the TPP. This would have limited the export prospects in the government procurement markets and pose difficulties to the 'Make in India' initiative, particularly because India uses government procurement as a tool to promote its manufacturing sector. A key feature of the TPP is the investor-state dispute settlement (ISDS) mechanism which allows private investors to seek remedies against a state in relation to breaches of investment provisions. This enables private investors to route their disputes to alternative bodies instead of domestic courts and would have had profound consequences for India. (Chatterjee, 2016)

The withdrawal of the US, in 2017, from the TPP (that accounted for 60 percent of trade within TPP) serves India's interests, since it limits the ability of the TPP to divert trade away from non-participating members like India. While participation in the TPP would have strengthened India's engagements with TPP members and strengthened its 'Indo-Pacific' narrative by side-lining China on economic and trade-related issues, it would have undermined our economic security and national interests.

Despite missing opportunities at some platforms, India has been actively engaged as a security provider in the region. With respect to that, India's defence and military actions in the region not only allow India to collaborate with other nations but also presents India with an opportunity to hone its military strategies.

India's Military Exercises-Creating the Edifice

- ***Malabar***

The bilateral India-US naval exercises that started in 1992, have slowly assumed a multilateral form with Australia and Japan joining the same. The Malabar exercises involve the conduct of simulated war games and manoeuvres. While Japan participated in the naval exercise in 2015, Australia which had initially joined in the 2007 exercise is participating in the exercises again this year after 13 years. The exercise is intended to send a strong message to China about the deterrence capabilities of these large navies.

While the Malabar exercise is formally independent of the Quad, the fact that all these four countries constitute the Quad adds to the potency of the message. In the words of Chief of Defence Staff General, Bipin Rawat, "Quad will ensure that the Indian Ocean Region and all other oceans around there is complete freedom of navigation, without fear of any other nation singularly trying to dominate the oceans." (Rej, 2020) Towards this objective, these exercises are proposed to be conducted in two phases- the first phase off the coast of Visakhapatnam and the second one in the Arabian sea.

The first phase of the exercise consisted of USS John S McCain, an Arleigh Burke-class destroyer led by the US Navy, Anzac-class HMAS Ballarat frigate led by the Australian Navy, JS Onami, a destroyer led by the Japanese Maritime Self Defence Force. Indian Navy was represented by a destroyer, a stealth frigate, an offshore patrol vessel, a fleet support ship, and a submarine, along with P-8I and Dornier maritime surveillance aircraft, an advanced trainer jet, and helicopters. Experts have stated that a more "credible line up" (Rej, 2020) was expected considering India-Australia naval exercise held in 2019, and previous editions of the exercise involved sophisticated anti-submarine warfare. (Rej, 2020)

- ***India- US joint military exercises***

The US has repeatedly emphasized on India's role in the Indo-Pacific in its "Indo-Pacific Strategy Paper" and the 2019 "Indo-Pacific Strategy Report". Prime Minister Narendra Modi emphasized upon the narrative of free, open, and inclusive Indo-Pacific during the Shangri La Dialogue in 2018 and recent elevation of Quad meetings to ministerial level reveal that India shares similar sentiments. Although India and the US have conducted joint exercises in the past, their recently held joint exercises must be seen in the context of efforts by both to enhance their defence and security cooperation due to convergence of interests.

The Indian Navy conducted the PASSEX joint exercise with the US Navy in the Indian Ocean in 2020. The exercise between the Indian Navy and the USS Nimitz aircraft carrier group was conducted near the Andaman and Nicobar Islands, near one of the busiest sea routes close to the Malacca Strait. The Nimitz carrier strike group consisted of USS Nimitz, Ticonderoga-class guided-missile cruiser USS Princeton and Arleigh Burke-class guided-missile destroyers USS Sterett and USS Ralph Johnson while Indian Navy warships comprised of INS Rana,

INS Sahyadri, INS Shivalik and INS Kamorta. The passage exercise, a sign of deepening strategic cooperation between India and the US in light of increasing tensions with China, only strengthens the Indian and US narratives of a "free and open Indo-Pacific." The growing complexity of US-India exercises is an indicator of shared strategic interests in a continuously changing Indo-Pacific. (Singh, 2020)

In 2019, India and US participated in their maiden tri-services humanitarian assistance and disaster relief (HADR) exercise that they have termed, "Tiger Triumph," in Visakhapatnam and Kakinada in Andhra Pradesh. The tri-military exercise would be conducted on an annual basis and signifies a development in the type of "joint military exercises that have been conducted on a bilateral level". Indian "naval ships Jalashwa, Sandhayak and Airavat; Indian Army troops from 19 Madras and 7 Guards; and Indian Air Force MI-17 helicopters and Rapid Action Medical Team (IAF-RAMT)" participated on behalf of India while the USS Germantown and troops from the U.S. 3rd Marine Division participated from the side of the US. The exercises were aimed at improving the interoperability between the forces of the two states, particularly when multiple countries respond to disasters. India and the US were able to successfully coordinate a humanitarian response to the 2005 Indian Ocean tsunami because they had participated and held numerous specific service-led military exercises. (Rajagopalan, 2019)

- ***India-Malaysia***

India's military and security outreach to the ASEAN countries has gained momentum in the changing Indo-Pacific and revolves around political dialogues, joint exercises, and security consultations. India and Malaysia share a history of cooperation in security and elevated their relations to that of strategic partners in 2010. Their strategic partnership is of significance with the shift from "Look East" to "Act East" policy. The Indian Navy participates in the Langkawi International Maritime and Aerospace Exhibition in Malaysia. The Indian Navy and Coast Guard are conducting port visits in light of Chinese naval footprint in the region.

In 2018, India conducted the "Harimau Shakti," a joint military exercise with Malaysia to promote interoperability between the armed forces of the two states and share their expertise of tactical counter-insurgency operations in jungle terrain of Sengai Perdik and Hulu Langat in Malaysia. The four Grenadiers Battalion of the Indian Army and the Royal Ranjr Regiment and Royal Malay Regiment from the Malaysian

Army participated in the exercise. While the exercise served to improve the counterinsurgency tactics of India and Malaysia, the larger objective was to strengthen their strategic partnership. (Rajagopalan, 2018)

India and Malaysia, in 2019, conducted a joint naval military exercise to test and strengthen their interoperability in the regions of South-East Asia and Western Pacific. Two of India's warships INS Sahyadri and INS Kiltan participated in the exercise. The naval exercise was conducted off the port of Kota Kinabalu, Malaysia. The harbor phases of the exercise involved official calls, social engagements, and interactions between the naval crews. ("India, Malaysia undertake joint naval exercise", 2019)

- ***India-Singapore-Thailand Naval Exercise***

The India Singapore Thailand trilateral exercise (SITMEX) was announced by Prime Minister Narendra Modi in Singapore during 2018 as part of his keynote address to the Shangri-La Dialogue. Since then, two exercises have been held- the first one in Andaman Sea in 2019 and the second one in the Andaman Sea hosted by the Republic of Singapore Navy in November 2020 (Rajagopalan, 2020).

While the SITMEX represents a growing number of India's naval engagements with various navies, it demonstrates that India is increasingly being considered and perceived as a maritime partner by regional navies and the willingness to strengthen their own efforts at a regional level instead of relying completely on the US to counter China. The SITMEX exercise strengthens India's strategic engagements under the Act East Policy on 2014.

India was represented by missile corvette INS Kora, guided missile destroyer INS Ranvir, P8I long-range maritime reconnaissance aircraft and Offshore Patrol Vessel Sumedha during SITMEX in 2019. In the SITMEX held in 2020, India was represented by "ASW (anti-submarine warfare) corvette Kamorta and missile corvette Karmuk" among others, Singapore was represented by "Formidable-class frigates, Intrepid and the Endeavour, an Endurance-class LST (landing ship tank)" and Thailand was represented by a "Chao Phraya-class frigate, the Kraburi". A statement released by India's Ministry of Defence stated that the exercise would include naval manoeuvres, surface warfare exercises and weapon firings (Rajagopalan, 2020).

These exercises have seen an impressive participation from the three navies during both editions of the edition of the SITMEX aimed at promoting mutual interoperability and assimilating "best practices" between the three navies. The fact that this year's exercise took place despite the COVID-19 pandemic shows the seriousness with which the three countries are pursuing these exercises.

Singapore and India have long pursued defence cooperation with their bilateral naval exercises SIMBEX continuing for more than 20 years now. The two countries first signed their defence cooperation agreement in 2003 and have since signed many more defence pacts. The defence relations between India and Thailand though not as old as those between India and Singapore have picked up in recent times with the holding of annual exercises involving army and air force and bi-annual maritime patrolling by both navies.

- ***MILAN***

The MILAN naval exercises, begun in 1995 in Port Blair, involved four ASEAN states and were started as an attempt to pacify South-East Asian states that were concerned about India's naval expansion programmes during the 1980s. Since then, the Indian Navy has conducted ten editions of the MILAN exercises under the theme of "synergy across the seas," and the exercise has expanded in its scale. The naval exercise is aimed at promoting interoperability, maritime security cooperation and reducing maritime risk at a multilateral level. The naval exercise is conducted under the aegis of the Eastern Naval Command and until 2018, was conducted at the Andaman and Nicobar Command. (Upadhyaya, 2020)

The 13th edition of MILAN was scheduled to take place in 2020 at the Indian Navy's Eastern Naval Command at Visakhapatnam but was cancelled due to the COVID-19 pandemic. India had invited 42 navies, including the US and Russia, except for China, Pakistan, Iraq and Yemen (who are dealing with internal conflict). Despite its cancellation, the fact that India had invited 42 navies and that it would have been one of the largest multinational naval exercises, demonstrates a shift in India's perception of the Indian Ocean.

- ***IONS -Indian Ocean Naval Symposium***

The Indian Ocean Naval Symposium (IONS), launched in 2008, by India is a biennial voluntary initiative that aims to promote and strengthen maritime cooperation among navies of littoral states of the Indian Ocean region (IOR) by serving as a forum for the discussion of relevant maritime issues. Since its launch in 2008, IONS has seen its membership grow by leaps and bounds with twenty-four member nations and eight observer states representing the littoral states of the Indian Ocean Region (Das, 2018). Since its inception, several seminars and workshops have been organized under the aegis of the IONS on a diverse range of topics such as maritime security, Humanitarian Assistance and Disaster Relief (HADR), collaborative capacity building etc. which reflect the objectives of the IONS.

Several maritime exercises have also been conducted by IONS, in the form of Search and Rescue naval drill conducted by India and China at the height of the Doklam crisis, under the aegis of the Bangladesh Navy. This demonstrates the success of the IONS in establishing itself as a non- controversial and non-political forum, unlike the QUAD, which has some political attributes.

Notwithstanding its non-political nature, the IONS is seen as a platform for India to build and deepen sustainable partnerships with the littoral states of the Indian Ocean region and thereby expand its sphere of influence in the region. IONS serves as a platform for fulfilling and promoting India's aim of establishing a rules-based and stable maritime order in the IOR free from security threats emanating from piracy and other terror threats but also from political influence of countries such as China which sought to build its power base in the region through its own bilateral initiatives (Das, 2018).

While India has played a leadership role in the establishment of the IONS and ensuring the expansion of its membership across the region representing South Asia, West Asia, South East Asia, Australia and East Africa, India needs to show a lot of political will in ensuring that this new found multilateral cooperation amongst the IOR countries is continued and the IONS achieves India's ambition of being a net security provider in the region and its requirement to ensure a rules based maritime order in the IOR which is crucial not only from a security standpoint but also is a critical towards developing economic prosperity.

- ***Regional Co-operation Agreement on Combating Piracy and Armed Robbery against Ships in Asia (RECAAP)***

"The Regional Cooperation Agreement on Combating Piracy and Armed Robbery against ships in Asia (ReCAAP) is the first regional government-to-government agreement to promote and enhance cooperation against piracy and armed robbery in Asia" ("About ReCAAP Information Sharing Centre |combating maritime robbery, sea piracy", n.d.). In light of the surging cases of piracy, hijacking and armed robbery in the late 1990's the then Japanese Prime Minister, Junichiro Koizumi, proposed the ReCAAP initiative in 2001, which aimed for multilateral cooperation among regional nations. (*Factsheet on the Regional Cooperation Agreement on Combating Piracy and Armed Robbery against Ships in Asia (RECAAP)*, n.d.) On November 29, 2006, the ReCAAP ISC (Information Sharing Centre) was established, which focused on facilitating communication and exchange of information among nations in order to combat armed robbery and piracy in the Asian waters. As of January 5, 2016, over 20 states have become contracting parties of ReCAAP, India being one of them (Win, Ahmed, Ansari, Masum & Jan, 2016). As a contracting party India, pursues cooperation with regards to information sharing, capacity building and cooperative agreements, which is institutionalised under ReCAAP ISC which is based in Singapore (ReCAAP Information Sharing Centre, n.d.).

The Indian Coast Guard (ICG) has been designated by the Government of India as a focal point for ReCAAP within India (Srivastava, n.d.). The ICG regularly conducts capacity building workshops in collaboration with ReCAAP. From June 19-20, 2019, the ICG co-hosted the 12th Capacity Building Workshop with ReCAAP ISC, which witnessed the participation of 31 international delegates from 19 countries, in addition to major national stakeholders and officials from state marine police, state maritime ports, etc (Ministry of Defence, 2019). Apart from that the ICG had also hosted workshops in November 2011, at Goa and in December of 2017 at New Delhi. So far, India has played an active role in collaborating with the organisation and has provided essential resources. However, the participation has been limited to certain agencies of the Indian Government.

- ***Malacca Straits Security Initiative***

The Malacca Straits Security Initiative (MSSI) or the Malacca Straits Sea Patrol (MSSP) was incepted in 2004 in the form of a quasi-quadrilateral agreement between Thailand, Malaysia, Singapore and Indonesia. The initiative aimed at coordinating patrols in the region which aimed at reducing piracy and smuggling activities in the adjacent waters. Over the years the initiative has expanded and today it comprises the Malacca Straits Sea Patrol (MSSP), the "Eyes-in-the-Sky" (EiS) Combined Maritime Air Patrols, along with the Intelligence Exchange Group (IEG) (Briefing, 2017).

Given that the Malacca straits connect the South China Sea to the Indian Ocean, as well as about 40 percent of India's trade goes through these waters, it holds immense strategic significance for India. As of 2018 India had sought to become a part of the Malacca Sea Patrol to carry out coordinated aerial and maritime patrols in the strait (Joshi,

2020). However, according to the discussions held between India and Indonesia regarding the matter, Indonesian counterparts stated that it would "not be feasible" for India to join the initiative. Despite the meetings held between the technical experts from both the nations, it was realised that India did not really understand the mechanisms of the MSP, thereby hindering its process to join the initiative (Mitra, 2018). But on the other hand, India and Indonesia released a joint statement (Ministry of External Affair: Media Center, 2018) in 2018, after a bilateral meeting was held between the leaders of both the nations, which discussed details of addressing common maritime concerns.

- ***India as a First Responder and Critical Player in the region***

India's efforts to address regional and international crises reflect its ever-increasing capabilities, sphere of influence and commitment and willingness as a responsible player in the global order. As the then Foreign Secretary Dr. S. Jaishankar put it, India's foreign policy aims "to aspire to be a leading power, rather than just a balancing power ... (and) a willingness to shoulder greater global responsibilities." India interprets the concept of a "first responder" (Ministry of External Affairs, n.d.) broadly and is accurately reflected in "global responsibilities" that it shoulders by responding to a variety of crises in the Indo-Pacific region and beyond.

- During the 2004 Tsunami, India provided relief and deployed assets to Sri Lanka and Maldives. Despite being severely affected, India initially declined and later accepted assistance from the UN and private agencies. "India deployed 14 Navy vessels, nearly 1,000 military personnel and several dozen helicopters and airplanes to Sri Lanka." (Embassy of India-Sweden and Latvia, 2015) This reflects India's desire to shift the narrative of India from that of aid recipient to that of donor (Ministry of External Affairs, n.d.).
- In 2007, following cyclone Sidr, India provided humanitarian aid to Bangladesh and Myanmar. India was one of the few countries that Myanmar accepted aid from. This reinforced India's principles of humanitarian and disaster relief (HADR) that place emphasis on sovereignty of the recipient (Ministry of External Affairs, n.d.).
- In 2015, following the earthquake that wrecked Nepal, India was quick to provide assistance through Operation Maitri, which involved numerous government agencies, the National

Disaster Response Force (NDRF) and NGO's. The central government provided around USD 18 million on disaster relief. In addition to deploying military assets, technical teams composed of structural engineering experts, post disaster needs assessment specialists, and power experts, were sent to restore grid lines (Ministry of External Affairs, n.d.).

- In 2017, Bangladesh and faced several crises, some of which were cyclone Mora and the ethnic conflict in the Rakhine state of Myanmar. Operation Insaniyat was initiated to provide assistance to Bangladesh and Myanmar with relief efforts towards the Rohingya refugees. India's aid to Myanmar between 2017-2019 amounted to USD 6.41 million. (Chakradeo, 2020)

In addition to providing bilateral aid and relief, multilateral forums that have been conceptualised and instituted by India have undertaken efforts in disaster management. The Bay of Bengal Initiative for Multi Sectoral Technical and Economic Cooperation (BIMSTEC) places emphasis on cooperation on "Environment and Disaster Management," with India as the lead country. The BIMSTEC Centre for Weather and Climate was established in 2014 and workshops have been conducted building disaster-warning systems for member countries. A BIMSTEC leaders retreat that was held in 2016 placed emphasis on strengthening cooperation on disaster management through joint exercises, resulting in the initiation of the BIMSTEC Disaster Management Exercise on the lines of SAADMEx. India hosted SAADMEx in 2017 and 2020. (Chakradeo, 2020)

Groupings such as IORA and the Indian Ocean Naval Symposium (IONS) engage a variety of maritime security issues, including HADR (Humanitarian aid and Disaster Relief). India chairs IORA's Core Group on Disaster Risk Management that led to the creation of a set of official guidelines for HADR. In 2019, India hosted the first cluster group of IORA members on disaster risk management. In the same year, IORA member state delegates participated in the annual HADR exercise. (Chakradeo, 2020)

However, India's contributions towards aiding its regional allies at the time of crisis has not just been limited to HADR during tsunamis, it also extends towards tackling non-traditional security challenges. One such example of this has been the deployment of 30 warships by the Indian Navy that, "escorted more than 1,500 ships and thwarted around thirty piracy attempts. India was a founding member of the Contact Group on Piracy off the Coast of Somalia (CGPCS) and led coordination efforts among different naval forces in the region" (Ministry of External Affairs, n.d.). Additionally, India has also provided assistance to Sri Lanka, Maldives and Bhutan to address foreign currency shortages through a currency swap mechanism that was instituted in 2012. Bearing in mind the current global pandemic, India has also extended assistance to its regional allies by lifting its ban on exports of drugs such as hydroxychloroquine and paracetamol. "In addition, medicines, including hydroxychloroquine and paracetamol were sent to South Asian Association for Regional Cooperation (SAARC) countries, as well as to Mauritius and the Seychelles. India has also provided medical aid to Caribbean and Latin American countries" (Jash, 2020).

8 Recommendations and Proposals

1. Even though in the recent past India's engagements with ASEAN and ASEAN nations have considerably improved, most of these negotiations have been on the lines of cultural and civilizational cooperation. These primarily include capacity building measures, and other human resource based developmental activities. The same can be said with respect to India's participation at IORA. From the six priority areas identified by IORA, India is a lead country for Disaster Risk Management and Academic, Science and Technology Cooperation and a part of the cluster group for Tourism, Maritime Safety and Security, Blue Economy and Women's Economic Empowerment. This leaves out important sectors of Trade and Investment facilitation and Maritime Security and safety. Thus, there is a need for India to play a more active role, especially with respect to these two sectors at regional forums (ASEAN, IORA) as it can substantially benefit India's own vision on the Indo-Pacific.
2. The notion of Quad Plus has seen limited participation, when it comes to the involvement of more regional actors. Considering its geographical location and its relations with Southeast Asian and South Asian nations, India should take a step to include other nations in the Quad Plus. This is with respect to both naval exercises and other deliberations organized by the informal forum.
    - India and its partners should focus on the maintenance of the rules based law and order, along with the foundational principles of democracy and other shared interests, which forms the basis of Quad. Moreover, India should also stress on establishing stronger relations with countries of the same democratic values like New Zealand and Canada to further invigorate its Indo-Pacific Policy.

- Additionally, apart from Quad, which is more political in nature, India should associate itself more closely with INOS (Indian Naval Ocean's Symposium), which experiences less political tensions. IONS can promote India's aim of a rules-based and stable maritime order in IOR by conducting regular maritime activities such as "Coordinated Patrols (CORPAT), Maritime Interdiction Operations, Search and Rescue Operations", and institutionalising them (Jash, 2020).

3. India's relations and associations with its smaller neighbours such as Bangladesh, Myanmar and Nepal have been more or less lopsided. Considering the nature of Indian investments seen in these nations in the past and its role as a security provider in the region, there still seems to be a mentality of India being too dominant among other regional nation states, after China. Nations like Myanmar, Nepal and Bangladesh are the most susceptible to China's debt-trap diplomacy. In the recent past too, there have been instances where China seems to have been influencing the domestic politics of these smaller states and has been seen introducing an anti-India narrative. This could be a serious security threat, as India shares a border with these nations. Bearing this in mind, it is imperative for India to cultivate better relations with the smaller countries. One way to do so, is to alter India's image in the eyes of these states, by providing them with equal say in bilateral or plurilateral forums. Coming up with policies similar to the India-Myanmar-Thailand trilateral highway, where it would benefit all sides. But while doing so India needs to be mindful of its assertive nature and that to give these smaller countries equal opportunities for participation and contribution.
4. The Pacific Island Countries are extremely important from a geostrategic point of view. Given India's policy of inclusivity and expansion of the Indo-Pacific region to the coast of Africa, it becomes essential for India to realize the potential of these small island states.
   - India has engaged in NSA level dialogues with Mauritius and Seychelles and considering the geographical locations of these nations their association with India would be of strategic interest from a security perspective. However, the major impediment to the NSA level dialogues have been the bilateral disputes among nations. In order to make the dialogues successful and improve the relations with Mauritius and Seychelles, India should encourage these states to keep their

bilateral differences aside and engage more dynamically to bolster the Indo-Pacific region.

- Furthermore, India's association with other small island nations that are resource rich have been limited. In order to improve its relations with the Pacific Island Countries, India should closely engage with individual nations while stressing on economic cooperation with these states. Considering the rich resource reservoirs that these islands states have, India could propose joint oil exploration exercises by employing its private sector industries to partner with fellow companies from these islands. Apart from that, introducing capacity building measures and assistance during natural disasters and aid for the health infrastructure (given the current pandemic) for these PIC nations, might aid in strengthening the relations between India and the small island states.

5. Bearing in mind the current COVID-19 pandemic, most nations are focusing their resources on combating the issue as well as devising ways to minimize the effects of the economic downturn that is to follow. India could use this opportunity to collaborate with other nations, which would aid India to form alliances who would help bolster India's Indo-Pacific vision in the future. India could aid smaller nations to build their health infrastructure and jointly work with larger nations to come up with vaccines and to share research on combating the virus.
6. With regards to the Free Trade Agreements with regional organizations like ASEAN, India has either not benefited adequately or the balance of trade seems skewed. The primary reason for this has been India's weak manufacturing sector. There needs to be serious effort to make the manufacturing sector export more competitively.
   - In addition, most of the FTAs presented to India remain underutilized, due to the limited knowledge among Indian exporters. There is a need to create more awareness among the Indian exporters so that they can make use of these opportunities and bolster the Indian economy. It is important to note that, at most times, the information regarding international trade collaborations or treaties are limited to the bigger companies of the nation. In order to reduce the unequal trade experienced due to the FTA, smaller industries should also be encouraged to take part in such initiatives.

7. Based on the above-mentioned points, it has been observed that India faces more difficulties with multilateral FTAs. Hence it would be in India's interest that it establishes FTAs with other countries on a bilateral level. India has faced some disagreements with Australia with regards to the dairy and agricultural industry. Hence in such cases, it is essential that both nations base their bilateral trade relations on areas of common interests. For instance, there is a large scope for New Zealand and India to promote their trade relations on multiple levels. India could benefit from New Zealand's expertise on the food processing industry, cold storage chains and the dairy sector, whereas in exchange, New Zealand could benefit from India's expertise on pharmaceutics. This would also be advantageous to India's Make in India initiative, as it would serve as a medium to share information and technological services.
8. India along with other willing countries should also work on Indo-Pacific document which must outline the Action plan for the next ten years and explore potential in defence, economic and political domains. Also, there is a serious need for a regular Indo-Pacific Summit which should look for Quick Impact Projects and work on common areas which would be for the benefit of the participating countries. Medicine, knowledge and education can be the three sectors for initial collaboration.
9. The Indo-Pacific region needs institutional support. India's entry into APEC (Asia-Pacific Economic Cooperation) and possible expansion of Indo-Pacific to include basic rules of engagement such as rules-based order and cooperation at times of disaster and logistical support would come handy for preparing the basic edifice. It may be worthwhile to look into Indo-Pacific treaty as envisaged by Marty Natalegawa, the former foreign minister of Indonesia.
10. India also needs to work on an Indo-Pacific plan. As Prime Minister Modi has envisaged the plan should work on integrating port networks and providing support for the shipping industry to connect the developmental dots. The region of Africa and Asia need support and mutual bonding on issues related to economic and political aspects.
11. The Quad can function as the bedrock of the Indo-Pacific theatre and Quad Plus could include other countries thereby enhancing its reach and support across the region. However, for Quad to become credible it would have to work on four-year plans in the field of

blue dot network, Indo-Pacific economic corridor and working on cyber and space utility aspects.

12. The Quad can work on a common intelligence network and also enhance development of software for military communication encryption and support research on critical futuristic areas such as quantum computing and developing safe and secure networks. For this purpose, the New Emerging Strategic Technologies division in MEA can work on a task force to identify focus areas.

References

- 11th ASEM Foreign Ministers' Meeting (FMM11) • ASEM InfoBoard. (2013). Retrieved 30 December 2020, from https://www.aseminfoboard.org/events/11th-asem-foreign-ministers-meeting-fmm11
- About ASEM and ASEM Education. Retrieved 30 December 2020, from https://www.asem-education.org/about
- About ReCAAP Information Sharing Centre |combating maritime robbery, sea piracy. Retrieved 1 January 2021, from https://www.recaap.org/about_ReCAAP-ISC
- Aneja, A. (2020). Europe Pivots Towards Indo-Pacific Amid Row with China - IDN-InDepthNews | Analysis That Matters. Retrieved 30 December 2020, from https://www.indepthnews.net/index.php/the-world/south-asia/3877-europe-pivots-towards-indo-pacific-amid-row-with-china
- Announcement of "Partnership for Quality Infrastructure: Investment for Asia's Future." Retrieved 31 December 2020, from https://www.mofa.go.jp/policy/oda/page18_000076.html
- ASEAN, India strengthen cooperation - ASEAN | ONE VISION ONE IDENTITY ONE COMMUNITY. (2020). Retrieved 31 December 2020, from https://asean.org/asean-india-strengthen-cooperation/
- Asia Africa Growth Corridor. (2017). *ASIA AFRICA GROWTH CORRIDOR Partnership for Sustainable and Innovative Development A Vision Document.* Ahemdabad: Africa Development Bank Meeting. Retrieved from https://www.eria.org/Asia-Africa-Growth-Corridor-Document.pdf
- Bagchi, I. (2020). India joins hands with NZ, Vietnam, S Korea to combat pandemic | India News - Times of India. Retrieved 30 December 2020, from https://timesofindia.indiatimes.com/india/india-joins-hands-with-nz-vietnam-s-korea-to-combat-pandemic/articleshow/74740424.cms
- Baruah, D. (2020). India in the Indo-Pacific: New Delhi's Theater of Opportunity. Retrieved 5 February 2021, from https://carnegieendowment.org/2020/06/30/india-in-indo-pacific-new-delhi-s-theater-of-opportunity-pub-82205
- Bhogal, P. (2018). *India-ASEAN economic relations: Examining future possibilities.* Retrieved from https://orfindiadefence.wordpress.com/2018/01/05/india-asean-economic-relations-examining-future-possibilities/
- Bhogal, P. (2020). *India-ASEAN economic relations: Examining future possibilities.* Retrieved from https://www.orfonline.org/research/india-asean-economic-relations-examining-future-possibilities/

- Briefing, I. (2017). Indian Navy Set to Patrol Malacca Straits Gateway to South China Sea - India Briefing News. Retrieved 1 January 2021, from https://www.india-briefing.com/news/indian-navy-set-patrol-malacca-straits-gateway-south-china-sea-13973.html/
- Chakradeo, S. (2020). *Neighbourhood First Responder: India's Humanitarian Assistance and Disaster Relief*. Brookings India. Retrieved from https://www.brookings.edu/wp-content/uploads/2020/08/HADR-Policy-Brief.pdf
- Chatterjee, P. (2016). A fine line: TPP and India - Gateway House. Retrieved 1 January 2021, from https://www.gatewayhouse.in/the-tpp-and-india-a-fine-line/
- Chatterji, S. (2017). North Korea's nuclear tests a threat to India's security: Sources. Retrieved 1 January 2021, from https://www.hindustantimes.com/india-news/north-korea-s-nuclear-tests-a-threat-to-india-s-security-sources/story-9EJkrf2Osb7nNlFCIn8FiL.html
- Chaudhury, D. (2019). Fourth edition of Quadrilateral meet this week in Southeast Asia. Retrieved 30 December 2020, from https://economictimes.indiatimes.com/news/politics-and-nation/fourth-edition-of-quadrilateral-meet-this-week-in-southeast-asia/articleshow/69571138.cms
- Chaudhury, D. (2019). PM Modi proposes Indo-Pacific Oceans Initiative. Retrieved 30 December 2020, from https://economictimes.indiatimes.com/news/politics-and-nation/pm-modi-proposes-indo-pacific-oceans-initiative/articleshow/71915838.cms?from=mdr
- Das, U. (2018). Indian Ocean Naval Symposium: Advancing India's Interests in the IOR. Retrieved 1 January 2021, from https://thediplomat.com/2018/11/indian-ocean-naval-symposium-advancing-indias-interests-in-the-ior/
- Embassy of India - Sweden and Latvia. (2015). *Responding First as a Leading Power*. Retrieved from https://www.indembassysweden.gov.in/page/responding-first-as-a-leading-power-by-mr-constantino-xavier/
- European Commission. (2018). *EU shapes its ambitious strategy on India*. Retrieved from https://ec.europa.eu/commission/presscorner/detail/en/IP_18_6481
- *Factsheet on the Regional Cooperation Agreement on Combating Piracy and Armed Robbery against Ships in Asia (RECAAP)*. Retrieved from https://www.mot.gov.sg/DATA/0/docs/ReCAAP%20factsheet%20_Nov06_%20%5BFINAL%5Das%20of%20281106.pdf
- Fillip to "Act East" as India joins key sub-regional group. (2019). Retrieved 30 December 2020, from https://www.outlookindia.com/newsscroll/fillip-to-act-east-as-india-joins-key-subregional-group/1588972
- Haidar, S. (2020). India and ASEAN to expand trade despite RCEP walkout. Retrieved 29 December 2020, from https://www.thehindu.com/news/national/prime-minister-narendra-modi-addresses-the-17th-india-asean-summit-through-videoconference/article33084299.ece
- Home - Mcommerce. Retrieved 29 December 2020, from https://commerce.gov.in
- How Much Trade Transits the South China Sea? | ChinaPower Project. (2017). Retrieved 1 January 2021, from https://chinapower.csis.org/much-trade-transits-south-china-sea/
- India, Japan review situation in Indo-Pacific; resolve to ramp up cooperation in third countries. (2019). Retrieved 31 December 2020, from https://economictimes.

indiatimes.com/news/defence/india-japan-review-situation-in-indo-pacific-resolve-to-ramp-up-cooperation-in-third-countries/articleshow/71888924.cms?from=mdr

- India, Malaysia undertake joint naval exercise. (2019). Retrieved 1 January 2021, from https://www.indiatoday.in/india/story/india-malaysia-undertake-joint-naval-exercise-1599122-2019-09-14
- India-Myanmar-Thailand Trilateral Highway - Maritime Gateway. (2019). Retrieved 29 December 2020, from http://www.maritimegateway.com/india-myanmar-thailand-trilateral-highway/
- India's Military Bilateral and Multilateral Exercises in 2019–A Compendium. (2019). Retrieved 6 February 2021, from https://www.vifindia.org/sites/default/files/India-s-Military-Bilateral-and-Multilateral-Exercises-in-2019.pdf
- Indian Ocean Rim Association discusses ways to achieve larger cooperation. (2019). Retrieved 30 December 2020, from https://www.thehindubusinessline.com/news/indian-ocean-rim-association-discusses-ways-to-achieve-larger-cooperation/article29918775.ece
- Indian Ocean Rim Association discusses ways to achieve larger cooperation | | Factly. (2019). Retrieved 30 December 2020, from https://factly.forumias.com/indian-ocean-rim-association-discusses-ways-to-achieve-larger-cooperation/
- Izzuddin, M. (2020). India has left RCEP behind, but not its ambition in Southeast Asia. Retrieved 29 December 2020, from https://www.lowyinstitute.org/the-interpreter/india-has-left-rcep-behind-not-its-ambition-southeast-asia
- Jaishankar, D. (2020). The Australia–India Strategic Partnership: Accelerating Security Cooperation in the Indo–Pacific. Retrieved 30 December 2020, from https://www.lowyinstitute.org/publications/australia-india-strategic-partnership-security-cooperation-indo-pacific
- Jash, A. (2020). COVID-19: Boosting Indo-Pacific Alignment and India's Regional Role. Retrieved 1 January 2021, from https://thediplomat.com/2020/06/covid-19-boosting-indo-pacific-alignment-and-indias-regional-role/
- Joshi, M. (2020). India and the Malacca conundrum | ORF. Retrieved 1 January 2021, from https://www.orfonline.org/research/india-and-the-malacca-conundrum/
- Joshi, Y. (2017). *India-Japan-Australia minilateral: The promise and perils of balancing locally.* ORF. Retrieved from https://www.orfonline.org/research/india-japan-australia-minilateral-the-promise-and-perils-of-balancing-locally/
- Khanna, A. (2020). UK plans new 5G club of 10 democracies, including India: Report. Retrieved 30 December 2020, from https://www.livemint.com/news/india/uk-plans-new-5g-club-of-10-democracies-including-india-report-11590759252503.html
- Kumar, M. (2019). Rejecting RCEP was the easy part |HT Analysis. Retrieved 1 January 2021, from https://www.hindustantimes.com/analysis/rejecting-rcep-was-the-easy-part-ht-analysis/story-oM0QORymKE5CGUZo9GEAPP.html
- Macron wants strategic Paris-Delhi-Canberra axis amid Pacific tension. (2018). Retrieved 31 December 2020, from https://www.reuters.com/article/us-australia-france/macron-wants-strategic-paris-delhi-canberra-axis-amid-pacific-tension-idUSKBN1I330F
- MEA Expands Indian Ocean Division to Include Islands off African Coast. (2019). Retrieved 31 December 2020, from https://thewire.in/external-affairs/

ministry-external-affairs-indian-ocean

- Medcalf, R., 2019. Indo-Pacific Visions: Giving Solidarity a Chance. *Asia policy*, [online] 14(3), pp.79–95. Retrieved from https://www.nbr.org/wp-content/uploads/pdfs/publications/ap14-3-medcalf-july2019.pdf
- Ministry of Armed Forces of France. (2019). *France and Security in the Indo-Pacific.* Retrieved from https://www.defense.gouv.fr/layout/set/print/content/download/532754/9176250/version/3/file/France+and+Security+in+the+Indo-Pacific+-+2019.pdf
- Ministry of Defence. (2019). *ICG co-hosts 12th ReCAAP ISC capacity building workshop in capital from June 19.* Retrieved from https://pib.gov.in/PressReleasePage.aspx?PRID=1574851
- Ministry of External Affairs. *Brief on ASEAN-India relations.* Ministry of External Affairs. Retrieved from https://www.indmissionasean.gov.in/pages/MTk
- Ministry of External Affairs. *Brief Note on India-Japan Bilateral Relations.* Retrieved from https://www.mea.gov.in/Portal/ForeignRelation/India-Japan_Bilateral_Brief_feb_2020.pdf
- Ministry of External Affairs, n.d. *ASEAN-India Relations.* [online] Retrieved from: https://mea.gov.in/Portal/ForeignRelation/ASEAN_India_August_2017.pdf
- Ministry of External Affairs. *Responding First as a Leading Power.* Retrieved from https://mea.gov.in/Portal/IndiaArticleAll/636548962666860480_Responding_First_Leading_Power.pdf
- Ministry of External Affairs Media Centre. (2012). *Joint Ministerial Statement on the 6th Mekong Ganga Cooperation Meeting.* Retrieved from https://www.mea.gov.in/press-releases.htm?dtl/20457/Joint+Ministerial+Statement+on+the+6th+Mekong+Ganga+Cooperation+Meeting
- Ministry of External Affair, Media Center: Bilateral/Multilateral Documents. (2013). *Outcome Document of the Second NSA-Level Meeting on Trilateral Cooperation on Maritime Security between India, the Maldives and Sri Lanka.* Retrieved from https://www.mea.gov.in/bilateral-documents.htm?dtl/21922/Outcome+Document+of+the+Second+NSALevel+Meeting+on+Trilateral+Cooperation+on+Maritime+Security+between+India+the+Maldives+and+Sri+Lanka
- Ministry of External Affair: Public Diplomacy. (2014). *NSA level meeting on trilateral Maritime Security Cooperation between India, Sri Lanka and Maldives.* Retrieved from https://www.mea.gov.in/in-focus-article.htm?23037/NSA+level+meeting+on+trilateral+Maritime+Security+Cooperation+between+India+Sri+Lanka+and+Maldives
- Ministry of External Affair, Media Center. (2015). *Joint Statement on India and Japan Vision 2025: Special Strategic and Global Partnership Working Together for Peace and Prosperity of the Indo-Pacific Region and the World (December 12, 2015).* Retrieved from https://www.mea.gov.in/bilateral-documents.htm?dtl%2F26176%2FJoint_Statement_on_India_and_Japan_Vision_2025_Special_Strategic_and_Global_Partnership_Working_Together_for_Peace_and_Prosperity_of_the_IndoPacific_R
- Ministry of External Affairs. (2016). *Mekong-Ganga Cooperation (MGC).* Retrieved from https://reconasia-production.s3.amazonaws.com/media/filer_public/e1/e1/e1e18a02-9384-4ac8-a487-46e9280728e4/mcg_n_2016_6thministerialmeeting.pdf

- Ministry of External Affairs. (2017). *About Asia-Europe Meeting (ASEM)*. Retrieved from https://mea.gov.in/aseanindia/about-asem.htm
- Ministry of External Affairs. (2017). *About Mekong-Ganga Cooperation (MGC)*. Retrieved from https://mea.gov.in/aseanindia/about-mgc.htm
- Ministry of External Affairs Media Center. (2017). *India-Australia-Japan-U.S. Consultations on Indo-Pacific (November 12, 2017)*. Retrieved from https://mea.gov.in/press-releases.htm?dtl/29110/IndiaAustraliaJapanUS_Consultations_on_IndoPacific_November_12_2017
- Ministry of External Affairs, (2017). *Non-Proliferation Order Related To UN Security Council Resolutions On DPRK*. Gazette of India. [online] Retrieved from: http://www.mea.gov.in/Uploads/PublicationDocs/29093_New_DGFT.pdf
- Ministry of External Affair: Media Center. (2017). *Official Spokesperson's response to a query on participation of India in OBOR/BRI Forum*. Retrieved from https://mea.gov.in/media-briefings.htm?dtl%2F28463%2FOfficial+Spokespersons+response+to+a+query+on+participation+of+India+in+OBORBRI+Forum
- Ministry of External Affairs: Annual Report. (2018). *Annual Report | 2018-19*. Ministry of External Affairs. Retrieved from http://www.mea.gov.in/Uploads/PublicationDocs/31719_MEA_AR18_19.pdf
- Ministry of External Affairs. (2018). *India-Australia-Japan-US Consultations*. Retrieved from https://www.mea.gov.in/press-releases.htm?dtl/29961/IndiaAustraliaJapanUS+Consultations
- Ministry of External Affair: Media Center. (2018). *India-Indonesia Joint Statement during visit of Prime Minister to Indonesia (May 30, 2018)*. Retrieved from https://www.mea.gov.in/bilateral-documents.htm?dtl/29932/IndiaIndonesia+Joint+Statement+during+visit+of+Prime+Minister+to+Indonesia+May+30+2018
- Ministry of External Affairs: Media Center. (2018). *India-Vietnam Joint Statement during State Visit of President to Vietnam*. Retrieved from https://www.mea.gov.in/bilateral-documents.htm?dtl/30615/IndiaVietnam_Joint_Statement_during_State_Visit_of_President_to_Vietnam
- Ministry of External Affair: Media Center: Press Release. (2018). *Press Release on State Visit of President to Madagascar (March 14–15, 2018)*. Retrieved from https://www.mea.gov.in/press-releases.htm?dtl%2F29637%2Fpress+release+on+state+visit+of+president+to+madagascar+march+1415+2018
- Ministry of External Affairs, Media Center: Press Release. (2018). *Visit of Minister of State for External Affairs General Dr. V.K. Singh (Retd.) to the Democratic People's Republic of Korea*. Retrieved from https://www.mea.gov.in/press-releases.htm?dtl/29899/Visit+of+Minister+of+State+for+External+Affairs+General+Dr+VK+Singh+Retd+to+the+Democratic+Peoples+Republic+of+Korea
- Ministry of External Affairs, Media Center. (2018). *Prime Minister's Keynote Address at Shangri La Dialogue (June 01, 2018)*. Retrieved from https://www.mea.gov.in/Speeches-Statements.htm?dtl%2F29943%2FPrime+Ministers+Keynote+Address+at+Shangri+La+Dialogue+June+01+2018
- Ministry of External Affairs. (2019). *11th Delhi Dialogue; 6th Indian Ocean Dialogue and associated events (December 13–14, 2019)*. Retrieved from https://mea.gov.in/press-releases.htm?dtl/32180/11th+Delhi+Dialogue+6th+Indian+Ocean+Dialogue+and+associated+events+December+1314+2019

- Ministry of External Affairs. (2019). *India-Australia-Japan-United States Consultations.* Retrieved from https://www.mea.gov.in/press-releases.htm?dtl/31403/IndiaAustraliaJapanUnited_States_Consultation
- Ministry of External Affairs Media Center. (2019). *Joint Ministerial Statement of the 10th Mekong-Ganga Cooperation Ministerial Meeting.* Retrieved from https://mea.gov.in/bilateral-documents.htm?dtl/31713/Joint+Ministerial+Statement+of+the+10th+MekongGanga+Cooperation+Ministerial+Meeting
- Ministry of External Affairs Media Centre. (2019). *Prime Minister's Speech at the East Asia Summit, 04 November 2019.* Retrieved from https://www.mea.gov.in/Speeches-Statements.htm?dtl/32171/Prime_Ministers_Speech_at_the_East_Asia_Summit_04_November_2019
- Ministry of External Affairs. (2019). *Prime Minister's Speech at the East Asia Summit, 04 November 2019.* Retrieved from https://www.mea.gov.in/Speeches-Statements.htm?dtl/32171/Prime_Ministers_Speech_at_the_East_Asia_Summit_04_November_2019
- Ministry of External Affairs. (2020). *ASEAN-India Connectivity: Mapping Pathways of Shared Prosperity.* Retrieved from http://www.mea.gov.in/Portal/IndiaArticleAll/636508288003662093_mea-blog-connectivity-ASEAN.pdf
- Ministry of External Affairs, India. (2020). *Foreign Secretary at Policy Exchange in London, UK (3rd November 2020)* [Video]. Retrieved from https://www.youtube.com/watch?v=sqFqmSW8sY8
- Ministry of External Affairs. (2020). *Foreign Secretary's Conference Call with counterparts from Indo-Pacific Countries.* Retrieved from https://mea.gov.in/press-releases.htm?dtl/32592/Foreign+Secretarys+Conference+Call+with+counterparts+from+IndoPacific+Countries
- Ministry of External Affairs. (2020). *Indo-Pacific Division Briefs.* Ministry of External Affairs. Retrieved from https://mea.gov.in/Portal/ForeignRelation/Indo_Feb_07_2020.pdf
- Ministry of External Affairs. (2020). *Joint Declaration on a Shared Vision for Maritime Cooperation in the Indo-Pacific Between the Republic of India and the Government of Australia.* Retrieved from https://mea.gov.in/bilateral-documents.htm?dtl/32730/Joint_Declaration_on_a_Shared_Vision_for_Maritime_Cooperation_in_the_IndoPacific_Between_the_Republic_of_India_and_the_Government_of_Australia
- Ministry of External Affairs; Media Center. (2020). *17th India-Vietnam Joint Commission Meeting.* Retrieved from https://www.mea.gov.in/press-releases.htm?dtl/32912/17th_IndiaVietnam_Joint_Commission_Meeting
- Ministry of External Affairs, Media Center. (2020). *ASEAN-India Ministerial Meeting.* Retrieved from https://www.mea.gov.in/press-releases.htm?dtl%2F32967%2FASEANIndia+Ministerial+Meeting
- Ministry of External Affairs, Media Center: Bilateral/Multilateral Documents. (2020). *Joint Statement on the third India-U.S. 2+2 Ministerial Dialogue.* Retrieved from https://www.mea.gov.in/bilateral-documents.htm?dtl/33145/Joint_Statement_on_the_third_IndiaUS_2432_Ministerial_Dialogue
- Ministry of External Affairs, Media Center. (2020). *Foreign Secretary's Speech at Policy Exchange.* Retrieved from https://mea.gov.in/Speeches-Statements.htm?dtl/33162/Foreign+Secretarys+Speech+at+Policy+Exchange

- Ministry of External Affairs, Media Center. (2020). *Fourth East Asia Summit (EAS) Conference on Maritime Security Cooperation.* Retrieved from https://mea.gov.in/press-releases.htm?dtl/32342/Fourth_East_Asia_Summit_EAS_Conference_on_Maritime_Security_Cooperation
- Ministry of External Affairs, Media Center. (2020). *Joint Statement on a Comprehensive Strategic Partnership between Republic of India and Australia.* Retrieved from https://www.mea.gov.in/bilateral-documents.htm?dtl%2F32729%2FJoint_Statement_on_a_Comprehensive_Strategic_Partnership_between_Republic_of_India_and_Australia
- Ministry of External Affairs; Media Center. (2020). *Prime Minister addresses 17th ASEAN India Summit.* Retrieved from https://www.mea.gov.in/press-releases.htm?dtl/33191/Prime+Minister+addresses+17th+ASEAN+India+Summit
- Mitra, D. (2018). Indonesia Told India Its Quest to Join Malacca Strait Patrols Isn't Feasible. Retrieved 1 January 2021, from https://thewire.in/diplomacy/india-indonesia-malacca-strait-patrol
- Mitra, D., & Srivas, A. (2020) India Wants to Urgently Review its ASEAN Goods FTA, But Other Countries Are Slow to Play Ball. Retrieved 1 January 2021, from https://thewire.in/trade/asean-goods-fta-india-rcep
- Mohan, C. (2015). Modi and the Indian Ocean: Restoring India's Sphere of Influence | Asia Maritime Transparency Initiative. Retrieved 31 December 2020, from https://amti.csis.org/modi-and-the-indian-ocean-restoring-indias-sphere-of-influence/
- Mukhopadhyay, A. (2020). CEPA: Fulcrum of future trade and economic relations? | ORF. Retrieved 1 January 2021, from https://www.orfonline.org/expert-speak/cepa-fulcrum-of-future-trade-and-economic-relations-61197/
- Nagda, A. (2019). India-Indonesia: A Natural Partnership for the Indo-Pacific. Retrieved 30 December 2020, from http://www.indiandefencereview.com/spotlights/india-indonesia-a-natural-partnership-for-the-indo-pacific/
- Nataraj, G. (2014). *India-Japan Economic Partnership Agreement: Gains and Future Prospects.* ORF. Retrieved from https://www.orfonline.org/research/india-japan-economic-partnership-agreement-gains-and-future-prospects/
- Panda, A. (2019). US, India, Australia, Japan 'Quad' Holds Senior Officials Meeting in Bangkok. Retrieved 31 December 2020, from https://thediplomat.com/2019/11/us-india-australia-japan-quad-holds-senior-officials-meeting-in-bangkok/
- Pandey, D. (2020). India's Outreach to Pacific Island Countries. Retrieved 1 January 2021, from https://diplomatist.com/2020/03/07/indias-outreach-to-pacific-island-countries/
- Panda, J. (2020). India and the 'Quad Plus' Dialogue. Retrieved 30 December 2020, from https://rusi.org/commentary/india-strategic-quad
- Panda, J. (2020). India's Ties to North Korea: Can New Delhi Overcome Challenges to Its Maturing Engagement? | 38 North: Informed Analysis of North Korea. Retrieved 1 January 2021, from https://www.38north.org/2020/09/jpanda093020/
- Panda, J. (2020). The Strategic Imperatives of Modi's Indo-Pacific Ocean Initiative. Retrieved 29 December 2020, from https://www.eastwestcenter.org/publications/the-strategic-imperatives-modi's-indo-pacific-ocean-initiative
- Pandey, P. (2020). India's Outreach to Pacific Island Countries. Retrieved 5 February 2021, from https://diplomatist.com/2020/03/07/indias-outreach-to-pacific-island-countries/

- Pant, H. (2016). South China Sea Ruling: Can This be India's Moment in the Indo-Pacific?. Retrieved 31 December 2020, from https://thediplomat.com/2016/07/south-china-sea-ruling-can-this-be-indias-moment-in-the-indo-pacific/
- Parameswaran, P. (2017). Why the New India-Singapore Naval Pact Matters. Retrieved 1 January 2021, from https://thediplomat.com/2017/11/why-the-new-india-singapore-naval-pact-matters/
- Paul, T. (2018). How India Will React to the Rise of China: The Soft-Balancing Strategy Reconsidered - War on the Rocks. Retrieved 31 December 2020, from https://warontherocks.com/2018/09/india-and-the-rise-of-china-soft-balancing-strategy-reconsidered/
- Peri, D. (2020). Australia to join Malabar naval exercise next month. Retrieved 31 December 2020, from https://www.thehindu.com/news/national/australia-to-join-malabar-naval-exercise-next-month/article32892277.ece
- *Plan of Action to Implement the ASEAN-India Partnership for Peace, Progress and Shared Prosperity (2016–2020).* (2020). Retrieved from https://asean.org/wp-content/uploads/images/2015/August/POA_India/ASEAN-India%20POA%20-%20FINAL.pdf
- *Plan of Action to Implement the ASEAN-India Partnership for Peace, Progress and Shared Prosperity (2021–2025).* (2020). Retrieved from https://asean.org/storage/2020/09/ASEAN-India-POA-2021-2025-Final.pdf
- Prasad, K. (2020). India ready to host Indo-Pacific Regional Dialogue next month. Retrieved 30 December 2020, from https://www.tribuneindia.com/news/nation/india-ready-to-host-indo-pacific-regional-dialogue-next-month-38366
- Prime Minister meets Pacific Island Leaders. (2019). Retrieved 31 December 2020, from https://pib.gov.in/PressReleseDetail.aspx?PRID=1586327
- Prime Minister of Japan and His Cabinet. (2015). *"The Future of Asia: Be Innovative" - Speech by Prime Minister Shinzo Abe at the Banquet of the 21st International Conference on the Future of Asia*. Retrieved from http://japan.kantei.go.jp/97_abe/statement/201505/0521foaspeech.html
- Pubby, M., & Chaudhury, D. (2018). Under pressure from South Korea, Modi government ends 8-year bonhomie with North Korea. Retrieved 1 January 2021, from https://economictimes.indiatimes.com/news/defence/no-indian-language-training-for-north-korean-soldiers/articleshow/58451142.cms?from=mdr
- Quad Meets Again, Discusses Rules-Based Order in 'Inclusive' Indo-Pacific. (2018). Retrieved 30 December 2020, from https://thewire.in/diplomacy/quad-meets-again-discusses-rules-based-order-and-inclusive-indo-pacific
- Rai, D. (2019). India's trade with its FTA partners: experiences, challenges and way forward. Retrieved 1 January 2021, from https://economictimes.indiatimes.com/blogs/et-commentary/indias-trade-with-its-fta-partners-experiences-challenges-and-way-forward/
- Rajagopalan, R. (2018). India, Malaysia Kick Off Military Exercise. Retrieved 1 January 2021, from https://thediplomat.com/2018/05/india-malaysia-kick-off-military-exercise/
- Rajagopalan, R. (2019). Growing India-South Korea Strategic Synergy: The Defense Domain. Retrieved 1 January 2021, from https://thediplomat.com/2019/09/growing-india-south-korea-strategic-synergy-the-defense-domain/

- Rajagopalan, R. (2019). Tiger Triumph: US-India Military Relations Get More Complex. Retrieved 1 January 2021, from https://thediplomat.com/2019/11/tiger-triumph-us-india-military-relations-get-more-complex/
- Rajagopalan, R. (2020). SITMEX: India-Singapore-Thailand Complete Second Trilateral Maritime Exercises. Retrieved 1 January 2021, from https://thediplomat.com/2020/11/sitmex-india-singapore-thailand-complete-second-trilateral-maritime-exercises/
- Ram, V. (2018). India's Defence Diplomacy with Southeast Asia An Impetus to Act East. *Institute For Defence Studies And Analyses, 12*(3), 55–78. Retrieved from https://idsa.in/system/files/jds/jds-12-3-2018-india-defence-diplomacy-with-southeast-asia-vram.pdf
- Rej, A. (2020). Expanded Malabar Exercise to Start on November 3. Retrieved 1 January 2021, from https://thediplomat.com/2020/10/expanded-malabar-exercise-to-start-on-november-3/
- Report by the ReCAAP Information Sharing Centre for the Ninth Meeting of the United Nations Open-ended Informal Consultative Process on Oceans and the Laws of the Sea. Retrieved 25 December 2020, from https://www.un.org/Depts/los/consultative_process/mar_sec_submissions/recaap.pdf
- Retired Indian Navy Commodore Venugopal Vengalil tweeted that a "more credible line up is required to send the right message to China if that is the intent,' as cited in Rej, A. (2020). Expanded Malabar Exercise to Start on November 3. https://thediplomat.com/2020/10/expanded-malabar-exercise-to-start-on-november-3/
- Sajjanhar, A. (2018). The India-ASEAN Partnership at 25 | Manohar Parrikar Institute for Defence Studies and Analyses. Retrieved 6 February 2021, from https://idsa.in/idsacomments/india-asean-partnership-at-25_asajjanhar_040118
- Second SYDP (SYDP-II) Workshop on Improving the Quality and Value of Fisheries Products for Food Security, Coastal Livelihoods – Indian Ocean Rim Association – IORA. Retrieved 30 December 2020, from https://www.iora.int/en/events-media-news/events/priorities-focus-areas/fisheries-management/2019/second-sydp-sydp-ii-workshop-on-improving-the-quality-and-value-of-fisheries-products-for-food-security-coastal-livelihoods
- Sen, R. (2017). What's needed for an India-NZ FTA to materialise. Retrieved 1 January 2021, from https://www.asiamediacentre.org.nz/opinion/rahul-sen-slow-road-to-india-nz-fta/
- Seshadri, V. (2014). Transforming Connectivity Corridors between India and Myanmar into Development Corridors. Retrieved 6 February 2021, from http://ris.org.in/images/RIS_images/pdf/Trans%20Report.pdf
- Seshadri, V. (2017). *India-Singapore CECA An Appraisal.* ASEAN- India Centre at RIS. Retrieved from https://www.ris.org.in/sites/default/files/INDIA_SINGAPORE_CECA.pdf
- Singh, A. (2019). India's South China Sea policy has not changed. Now, as before, there's no appetite to challenge China | ORF. Retrieved 1 January 2021, from https://www.orfonline.org/research/indias-south-china-sea-policy-has-not-changed-now-as-before-theres-no-appetite-to-challenge-china-55495/
- Singh, R. (2020). 8 Indian,US warships conduct maritime drills in Indian Ocean. Retrieved 1 January 2021, from https://www.hindustantimes.com/

india-news/8-indian-us-warships-conduct-maritime-drills-in-indian-ocean/story-WwAcbU0FyKbrwcJLr05aGP.html

- Sri Lanka upset with Mauritius over rights resolution. (2014). Retrieved 31 December 2020, from https://www.business-standard.com/article/news-ians/sri-lanka-upset-with-mauritius-over-rights-resolution-114030600721_1.html
- Srivastava, D. Indian Coast Gurad Merry Time!. Retrieved 1 January 2021, from http://sainiksamachar.nic.in/englisharchives/2007/feb01-07/h5.htm
- Takenori, H. (2018). The Free and Open Indo-Pacific Strategy: India's Wary Response. Retrieved 31 December 2020, from https://www.nippon.com/en/currents/d00436/
- The White House Office of the Press Secretary. (2015). *U.S.-India Joint Strategic Vision for the Asia-Pacific and Indian Ocean Region*. Retrieved from https://obamawhitehouse.archives.gov/the-press-office/2015/01/25/us-india-joint-strategic-vision-asia-pacific-and-indian-ocean-region
- Upadhyaya, S. (2020). India's Cancelled MILAN 2020 Exercise and Delhi's View of the Indian Ocean. Retrieved 1 January 2021, from https://thediplomat.com/2020/03/indias-cancelled-milan-2020-exercise-and-delhis-view-of-the-indian-ocean/
- Venkataramakrishnan, R. (2020). What you need to know about the India-US 2+2 dialogue and their efforts to deal with China. Retrieved 31 December 2020, from https://scroll.in/global/976926/what-you-need-to-know-about-the-india-us-2-2-dialogue-and-their-efforts-to-deal-with-china
- Vietnam important for India's Indo-Pacific Ocean's Initiative: Senior diplomat. (2020). Retrieved 29 December 2020, from https://economictimes.indiatimes.com/news/defence/vietnam-important-for-indias-indo-pacific-oceans-initiative-senior-diplomat/articleshow/78770772.cms?from=mdr
- Wadhwa, A. (2019). India and the South Pacific. Retrieved 1 January 2021, from https://www.isas.nus.edu.sg/wp-content/uploads/2019/04/ISAS-Insights-No.-562-India-and-the-South-Pacific.pdf
- Win, K., Ahmed, H., Ansari, A., Masum, A., & Jan, N. (2016). Critical Analysis of the Efficacy of the ReCAAP in Combating Piracy and Armed Robbery against Ships in Asia. *Journal Of The Indian Law Institute*, *58*(2) (April–June 2016), 160–188. Retrieved from https://www.jstor.org/stable/45163274?seq=1

The Authors

Dr. Pankaj K Jha is Associate Professor and Associate Dean of Research, as well as the Director for Centre for Security Studies at the Jindal School of International Affairs, O.P. Jindal Global University. He was the Director (Research) with Indian Council of World Affairs for more than two and half years. He had worked as Deputy Director with National Security Council Secretariat (2012-2013) and was closely associated with national security apparatus in India.

Ms. Kritika Karmakar is Undergraduate student at O.P. Jindal Global University and Centre Coordinator at the Centre for Security Studies. She has worked on publications concerning terrorism, South China Sea dispute and the Indo-Pacific. Her research interests lie in the field of security and strategic studies, psychology and international relations.

Mr. Joseph Punnen, is currently pursuing an undergraduate degree in Global Affairs and is a Research Assistant at the Centre for Security Studies. His areas of research interests include various security issues across Asia and the Americas. He is also an avid follower of Global Politics, whilst working on a research paper based on Russia's activities in the Arctic and its future.

Ms. Medha Mythili Nibhanupudi is Masters Student at O.P. Jindal Global University and was a Research Intern at Centre for Security Studies. Her research interest lies in the fields of non-traditional security issues such as energy security and humanitarian aid.

Ms. Grace Cheema is Masters Student at O.P. Jindal Global University and was a Research Intern at Centre for Security Studies. Her research interests vary from National Security Studies, Geo-economic studies, India-China Relations and International Relations.